creating spreadsheets
and charts in Excel

Visual QuickProject Guide

by Maria Langer

Peachpit Press

Visual QuickProject Guide
Creating Spreadsheets and Charts in Excel
Maria Langer

Peachpit Press
1249 Eighth Street
Berkeley, CA 94710
510/524-2178
800/283-9444
510/524-2221 (fax)

Find us on the World Wide Web at: www.peachpit.com
To report errors, please send a note to errata@peachpit.com
Peachpit Press is a division of Pearson Education

Copyright © 2005 by Maria Langer

Editor: Nancy Davis
Production Editors: Connie Jeung-Mills, Lisa Brazieal
Proofreader: Ted Waitt
Compositor: Maria Langer
Indexer: Julie Bess
Cover design: The Visual Group with Aren Howell
Interior design: Elizabeth Castro
Cover photo credit: PictureQuest

Notice of Rights
All rights reserved. No part of this book may be reproduced or transmitted in any form by any means, electronic, mechanical, photocopying, recording, or otherwise, without the prior written permission of the publisher. For information on getting permission for reprints and excerpts, contact permissions@peachpit.com.

Notice of Liability
The information in this book is distributed on an "As Is" basis, without warranty. While every precaution has been taken in the preparation of the book, neither the author nor Peachpit Press shall have any liability to any person or entity with respect to any loss or damage caused or alleged to be caused directly or indirectly by the instructions contained in this book or by the computer software and hardware products described in it.

Trademarks
Visual QuickProject Guide is a registered trademark of Peachpit Press, a division of Pearson Education.
All other trademarks are the property of their respective owners.

Throughout this book, trademarks are used. Rather than put a trademark symbol with every occurrence of a trademarked name, we state that we are using the names in an editorial fashion only and to the benefit of the trademark owner with no intention of infringement of the trademark. No such use, or the use of any trade name, is intended to convey endorsement or other affiliation with this book.

ISBN 0-321-25582-8

9 8 7 6 5 4 3 2 1

Printed and bound in the United States of America

To Timothy Clam,
for making my summer
so memorable

Special Thanks to…

Nancy Davis, for thinking of me for the Visual QuickProject series. And for remaining somewhat calm when I missed deadlines (sorry!) and pressure began to build.

Ted Waitt, for making sure I dotted my i's and crossed my t's.

Connie Jeung-Mills and Lisa Brazieal, for helping me fine-tune the book's layout and appearance.

Julie Bess, for delivering yet another great index on short notice.

Microsoft Corporation, for continuing to improve the world's best spreadsheet program for Windows and Macintosh users.

To Mike, for the usual things.

contents

introduction ix

| what you'll create | x | the web site | xiv |
| how this book works | xii | the next step | xv |

1. meet microsoft excel 1

learn the lingo	2	scroll a window	8
mouse around	3	choose from a menu	9
start or open excel	4	use a toolbar	10
look at excel (Windows)	5	have a dialog	11
look at excel (Mac OS)	6	exit or quit excel	12
change the view	7	extra bits	13

2. create the workbook file 15

create the workbook	16	save the workbook (Windows)	19
set view options (Windows)	17	save the workbook (Mac OS)	20
set view prefs (Mac OS)	18	extra bits	21

3. build the budget worksheet 23

name the sheet	24	enter column headings	29
understand references	25	make a column wider	30
enter information	26	enter values	31
activate a cell	27	calculate a difference	33
enter row headings	28	calculate a percent diff	34

v

contents

3. build the budget worksheet (cont'd)

sum some values	35	use the fill handle	40
calculate net income	37	change a value	43
copy formulas	38	extra bits	44
copy and paste	39		

4. duplicate the worksheet   49

copy the sheet	50	delete a row	54
clear the values	51	enter new values	55
insert a row	53	extra bits	57

5. consolidate the results   59

prepare the sheet	60	calculate percent diff	66
consolidate	61	extra bits	67
check the consolidation	65		

6. format worksheets   69

set font formatting	70	add borders	80
format values	72	apply shading	82
format percentages	74	change text color	84
set column widths	76	format all worksheets	85
set alignment	78	extra bits	86
indent text	79		

contents

7. add a chart — 89

hide a row	90
start the chart wizard	91
select a chart type	92
check the source data	93
set chart options	94
set the chart location	96
explode a pie	97
add data labels	99
extra bits	101

8. print your work — 103

select the sheets	104
open page setup	105
set page options (Windows)	106
set page options (Mac OS)	107
adjust margins	108
add a standard footer	109
add a custom header	110
save settings	113
preview the sheets (Win)	114
preview the sheets (Mac)	115
print your work (Windows)	116
print your work (Mac OS)	117
extra bits	118

index — 119

introduction

This Visual QuickProject Guide offers a unique way to learn about new technologies. Instead of drowning you in theoretical possibilities and lengthy explanations, this Visual QuickProject Guide uses big, color illustrations coupled with clear, concise step-by-step instructions to show you how to complete a specific project in a matter of hours.

Our project in this book is to create an Excel workbook file that compares actual to budgeted income and expenses for three months, consolidates the results, and illustrates consolidated expenses as a pie chart. Although our example uses income and expense items for a fictional business, you can easily customize the worksheets for your own business or personal use. For example, you can create a worksheet that compares your personal budgeted and actual expenditures to see how well you're keeping to your budget. Or use the skills you'll learn throughout this book to keep track of your business's customer invoices and payments.

As you work through the project, you'll learn how to build worksheet files from the ground up, enter data and formulas, and copy formulas to save time. You'll see how powerful and flexible Excel is by working through examples that show off its most commonly used features. You'll try out Excel's consolidation feature and create and "explode" a colorful, three-dimensional chart. You'll also fine-tune the appearance of your worksheet files by applying all kinds of formatting. Along the way, you'll get plenty of ideas for how you can use Excel to crunch the numbers in your life.

what you'll create

Create a worksheet file that compares budgeted to actual income and expenses for a full month.

Item Name	Budget	Actual	Difference	% Diff
Income Items				
Sales	8200	9103	903	0.11012195
Interest Income	100	83	-17	-0.17
Other Income	200	115	-85	-0.425
Total Income	8500	9301	801	0.09423529
Expense Items				
Automobile	150	182	32	0.21333333
Bank Fees	25	25	0	0
Contributions	30	50	20	0.66666667
Depreciation	300	300	0	0
Insurance	120	120	0	0
Interest Expense	75	94	19	0.25333333
Office Supplies	200	215	15	0.075
Postage	360	427	67	0.18611111
Professional Fees	180	180	0	0
Rent	1200	1200	0	0
Repairs	120	245	125	1.04166667
Taxes	360	365	5	0.01388889
Telephone	275	209	-66	-0.24
Travel & Entertainment				
Entertainment	500	412	-88	-0.176
Meals	250	342	92	0.368
Travel	600	269	-331	-0.5516667
Utilities	800	741	-59	-0.07375
Other Expenses	150	248	98	0.65333333
Total Expenses	5695	5624	-71	-0.0124671
Net Income	2805	3677	872	0.31087344

Duplicate the worksheet and modify the duplicates for two other months.

Create a consolidation that combines all information with live links to the source data.

	Budget	Actual	Difference	% Diff
Income Items				
Sales	27200	28312	1112	0.04088235
Interest Income	450	371	-79	-0.1755556
Other Income	700	496	-204	-0.2914286
Total Income	28350	29179	829	0.02924162
Expense Items				
Automobile	590	660	70	0.11864407
Bank Fees	75	87	12	0.16
Contributions	230	380	150	0.65217391
Depreciation	900	900	0	0
Insurance	520	520	0	0
Interest Expense	250	343	93	0.372
Office Supplies	1000	1106	106	0.106
Postage	1240	1423	183	0.14758065
Professional Fees	730	1230	500	0.68493151
Rent	3600	3600	0	0
Repairs	450	1141	691	1.53555556
Taxes	1080	1135	55	0.05092593
Telephone	850	1169	319	0.37529412
Travel & Entertainment				
Entertainment	1400	1217	-183	-0.1307143
Annual Party	1800	2513	713	0.39611111
Meals	600	787	187	0.31166667
Travel	1500	794	-706	-0.4706667
Utilities	2800	3430	630	0.225
Other Expenses	300	932	632	2.10666667
Total Expenses	19915	23367	3452	0.17333668
Net Income	8435	5812	-2623	-0.3109662

introduction

Format the worksheets so they look great when printed.

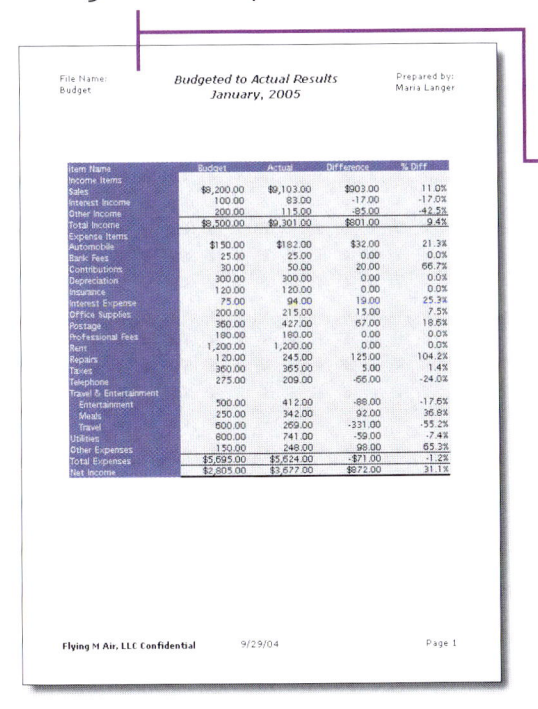

Print your worksheets, with custom headers and footers.

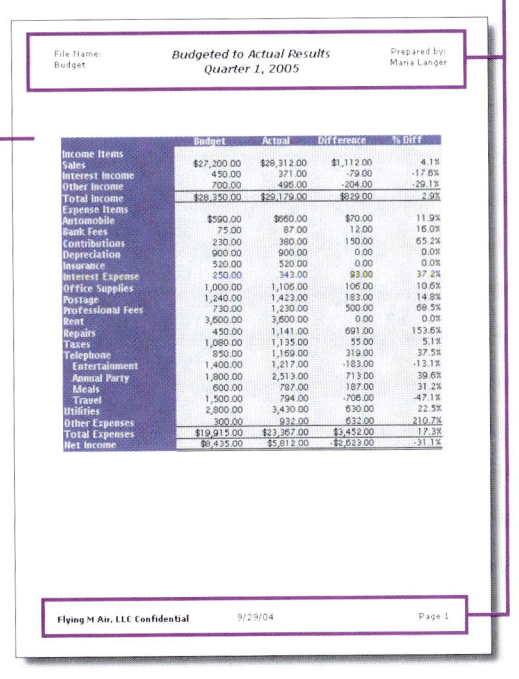

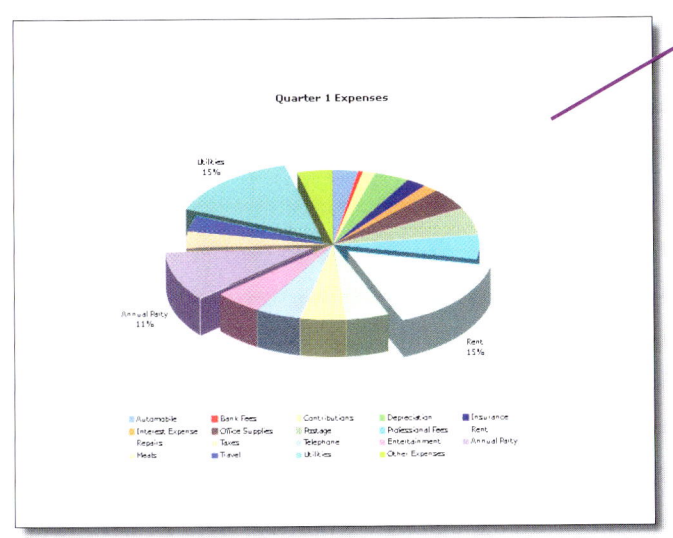

Create a colorful, "exploded" pie chart of consolidated expenses.

introduction

xi

how this book works

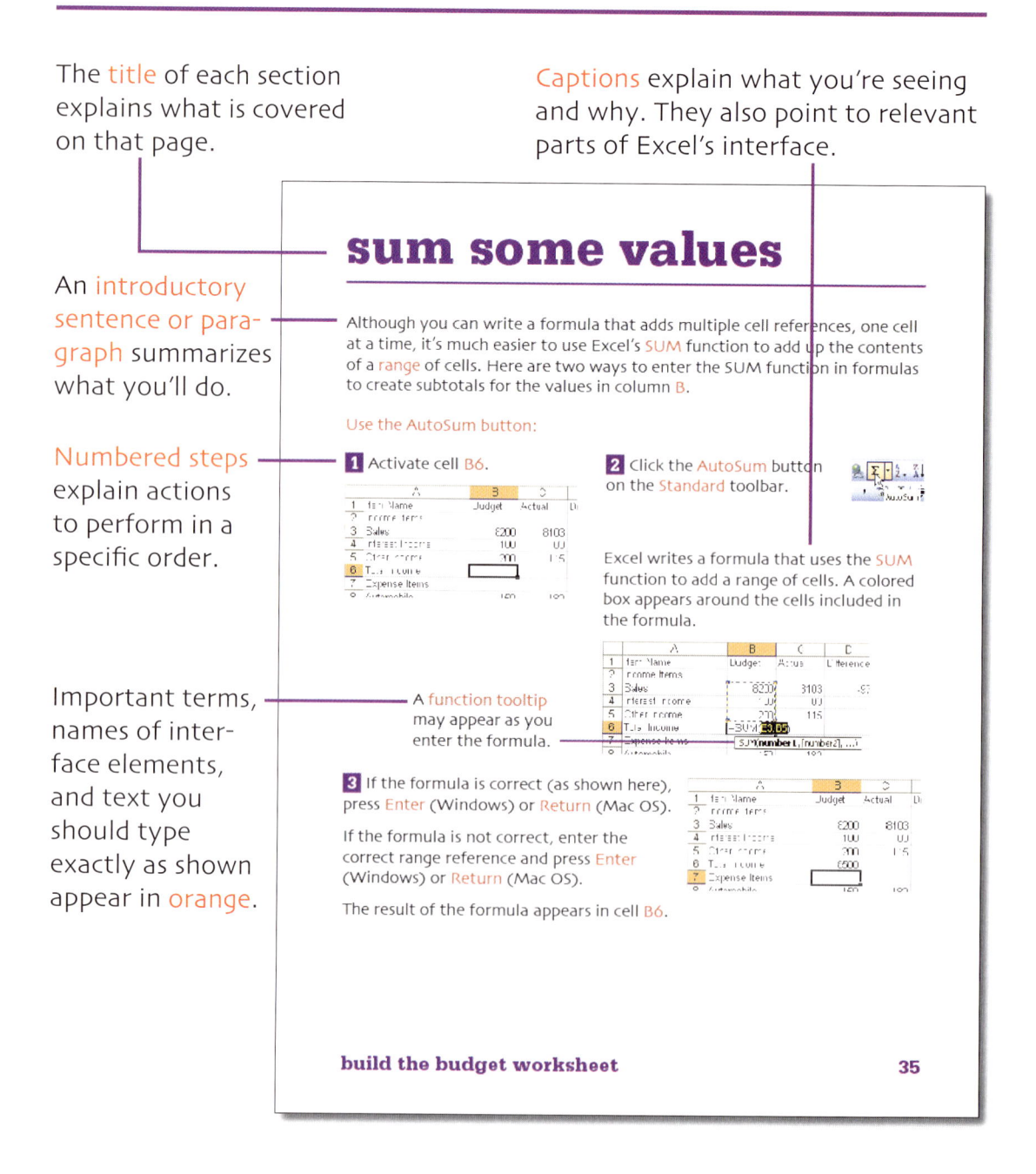

The *title* of each section explains what is covered on that page.

An *introductory sentence or paragraph* summarizes what you'll do.

Numbered steps explain actions to perform in a specific order.

Important terms, names of interface elements, and text you should type exactly as shown appear in *orange*.

Captions explain what you're seeing and why. They also point to relevant parts of Excel's interface.

---

sum some values

Although you can write a formula that adds multiple cell references, one cell at a time, it's much easier to use Excel's SUM function to add up the contents of a range of cells. Here are two ways to enter the SUM function in formulas to create subtotals for the values in column B.

Use the AutoSum button:

1 Activate cell B6.

2 Click the AutoSum button on the Standard toolbar.

Excel writes a formula that uses the SUM function to add a range of cells. A colored box appears around the cells included in the formula.

A function tooltip may appear as you enter the formula.

3 If the formula is correct (as shown here), press Enter (Windows) or Return (Mac OS).

If the formula is not correct, enter the correct range reference and press Enter (Windows) or Return (Mac OS).

The result of the formula appears in cell B6.

build the budget worksheet   35

---

xii   introduction

The extra bits section at the end of each chapter contains additional tips and tricks that you might like to know—but that aren't absolutely necessary.

enter values — The heading for each group of tips matches the section title.

extra bits

name the sheet p. 24
- As you'll see in Chapter 8, you can instruct Excel to automatically display a sheet name in a printed report's header or footer. That's a good reason to give a sheet an appropriate name.

activate a cell p. 27
- When you use the point-and-click method for activating a cell, you must click. If you don't click, the cell pointer won't move and the cell you're pointing to won't be activated.

enter row headings p. 28
- When you enter text in a cell, Excel's AutoComplete feature may suggest entries based on previous entries in the column.

14	Office Supplies
15	Postage
16	Postage
17	

  To accept an entry, press Enter (Windows) or Return (Mac OS) when it appears. Otherwise, just keep typing what you want to enter. The AutoComplete suggestion will eventually go away.

make a column wider p. 30
- You can't change the width of a single cell. You must change the width of the entire column the cell is in.

enter values pp. 31-32 — The page number(s) next to the heading makes it easy to refer back to the main content.
- You can enter any values you like in this step. But if you enter the same values I do, you can later compare the results of your formulas to mine to make sure the formulas you enter in the next step are correct.
- Do not include currency symbols or commas when entering values. Doing so will apply number formatting. I explain how to format cell contents, including values, in Chapter 6.
- If you use the arrow keys to move from one cell to the next, the selection area disappears. Although you can enter values without a selection area, using a selection area makes it easier to move from one cell to another.
- If, after entering values, you discover that one of the values is incorrect, activate the cell with the incorrect value, enter the correct value, and press Return or Enter to save it.

44   **build the budget worksheet**

introduction   **xiii**

the web site

Find this book's companion Web site at:
http://www.langerbooks.com/excelquickproject/.

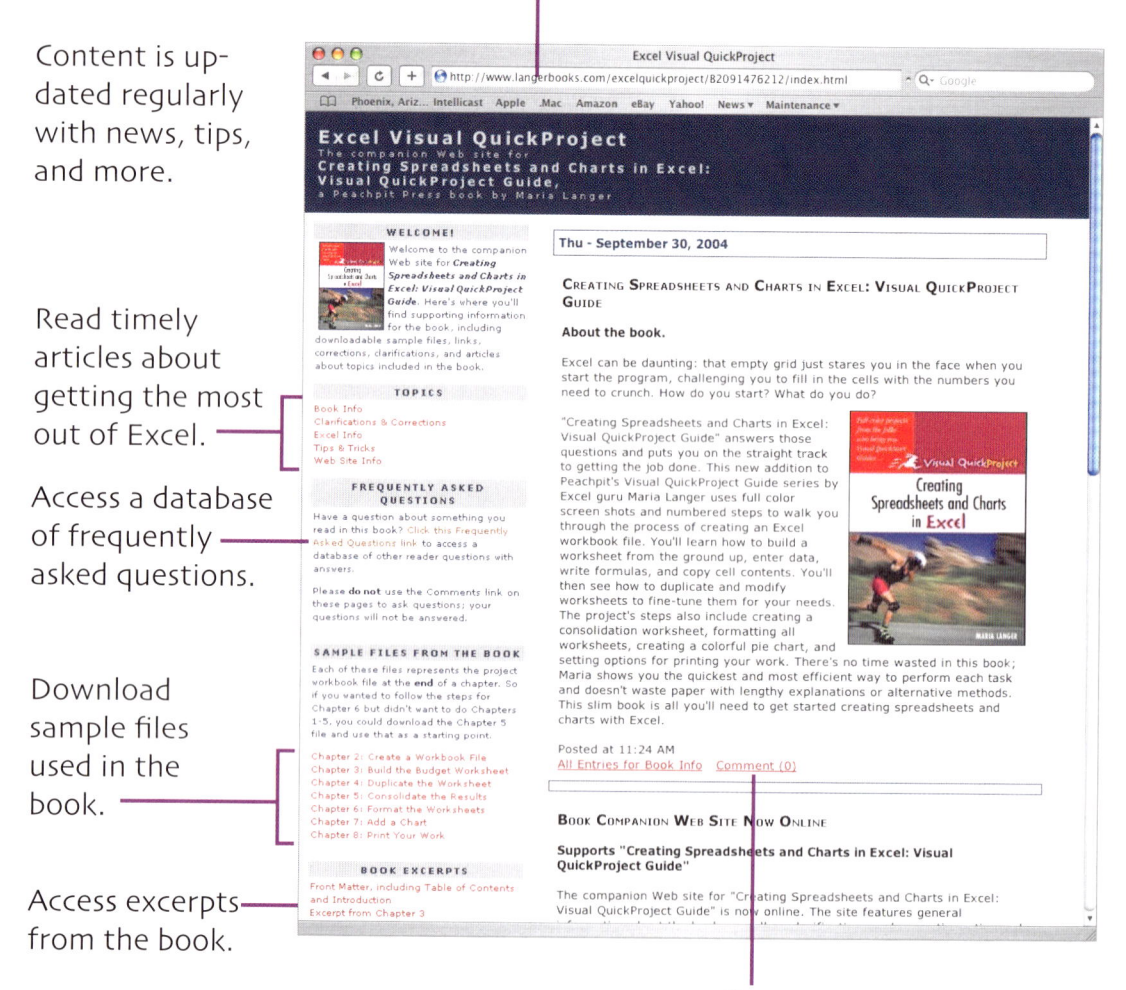

Content is updated regularly with news, tips, and more.

Read timely articles about getting the most out of Excel.

Access a database of frequently asked questions.

Download sample files used in the book.

Access excerpts from the book.

Share your comments and tips with other site visitors.

xiv introduction

the next step

While this Visual QuickProject Guide will walk you through all of the steps required to create and format worksheets and charts, there's more to learn about Excel. After you complete this project, consider picking up one of my books about Excel—*Microsoft Office Excel 2003 for Windows: Visual QuickStart Guide* or *Microsoft Excel X for Macintosh: Visual QuickStart Guide*—as a handy, in-depth reference.

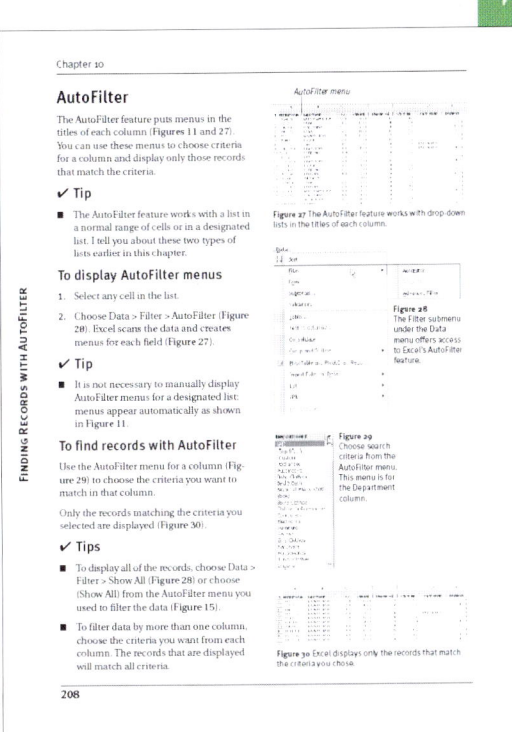

Both books include more advanced information about using Excel to create worksheets, lists, and charts. They tell you about all the options you see in Excel dialogs, explain how to customize Excel so it works the way you need it to, and provide detailed, step-by-step instructions for using basic, intermediate, and advanced Excel features.

introduction   **xv**

1. meet microsoft excel

Microsoft Excel is a full-featured spreadsheet program that you can use to create worksheets and charts like the ones you'll create with this book.

As you work with Excel, you'll see that it has a lot of the same interface elements you're familiar with from using your other Windows or Mac OS programs: windows, menus, dialogs, and buttons. And, as you work your way through this book you'll see that the Windows and Mac OS versions of Excel are remarkably similar—so similar that instructions for one version of the program usually work for the other.

In this chapter, I introduce you to Excel's interface elements and tell you about the techniques you'll need to know to use Excel. If this project is your first hands-on experience with Excel or your computer, be sure to read through this chapter!

This book covers Excel 2003 for Windows…

…and Excel 2004 for Macintosh.

But if you have an earlier version of Excel, you should still be able to follow most of the instructions in this book.

1

learn the lingo

Before you start working with Excel, let me review a few of the terms I'll use throughout this book. If you've been working with your computer for a while, this may seem a bit basic, but I do want to make sure we're on the same page (so to speak) as we work through this project.

Windows Explorer is the Windows program that you use to work with files.

If you need to learn more about using Windows, be sure to check out Windows XP: Visual QuickStart Guide by Chris Fehily.

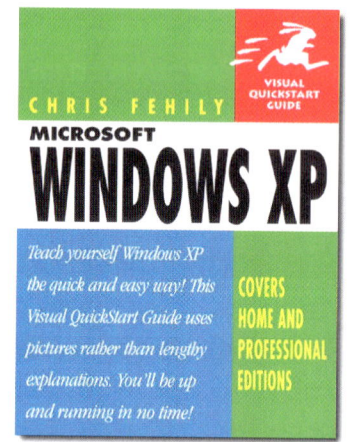

An icon is a graphical representation of a file.

EXCEL   Microsoft Excel

Here's what the Excel program icons look like in Windows (left) and Mac OS X (right).

Budget   Budget

And here's what an Excel document icon looks like in Windows (left) and Mac OS X (right).

Finder is the Mac OS program that you use to work with files.

If you need to learn how to use Mac OS X, check out Mac OS X Panther: Visual QuickStart Guide by Maria Langer. (Yes, that's me.)

2   meet microsoft excel

mouse around

The white (Windows) or black (Mac OS) arrow that appears on your screen is the mouse pointer. Move your mouse and the mouse pointer moves.

Point means to position the tip of the mouse pointer on something. For example, you can point to a menu,...

...or point to a button.

The mouse pointer can also change its appearance when you point to other things. For example, if you point to a cell in an Excel worksheet window, it changes into a cross pointer...

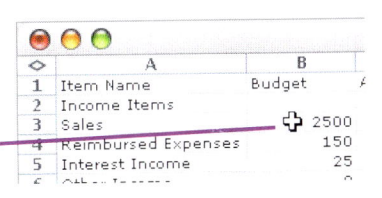

...and if you point to a column heading in an Excel worksheet window, it changes to an arrow pointing down.

You use the button(s) on your mouse to click, double-click, and drag.

Click means to press and release the left button on a Windows mouse or the only button on a Mac OS mouse.

Right-click means to press and release the right button on a Windows mouse. (You can't right-click on a Mac unless your Mac has a two-button mouse.)

Double-click means to click twice fast—without moving the mouse between clicks.

Drag means to point to something, hold the mouse button down, and move the mouse. You use this technique to move icons, select text, and perform other tasks.

A typical Windows mouse has two buttons.

A standard Mac OS mouse has only one button. On the Apple Pro Mouse shown here, the whole top of the mouse is a button.

meet microsoft excel

start or open excel

In Windows, you *start* a program. In Mac OS, you *open* a program. To keep things simple, I'll use the word *start* for both platforms.

In Windows:

1 Click Start to display the Start menu.

2 Click All Programs.

3 Click Microsoft Office.

4 Click Microsoft Office Excel 2003.

Excel starts and an untitled workbook window appears, as shown on page 5.

In Mac OS:

1 Double-click your hard disk icon to open its window.

2 Double-click Applications.

3 Double-click Microsoft Office 2004.

4 Double-click Microsoft Excel.

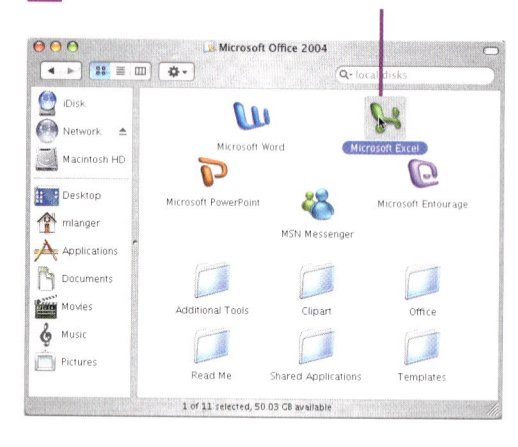

Excel starts. If a Project Gallery window appears, click Cancel to dismiss it. An untitled workbook window appears, as shown on page 6.

4   meet microsoft excel

look at excel (Windows)

Here are some of the important interface elements in Excel for Windows.

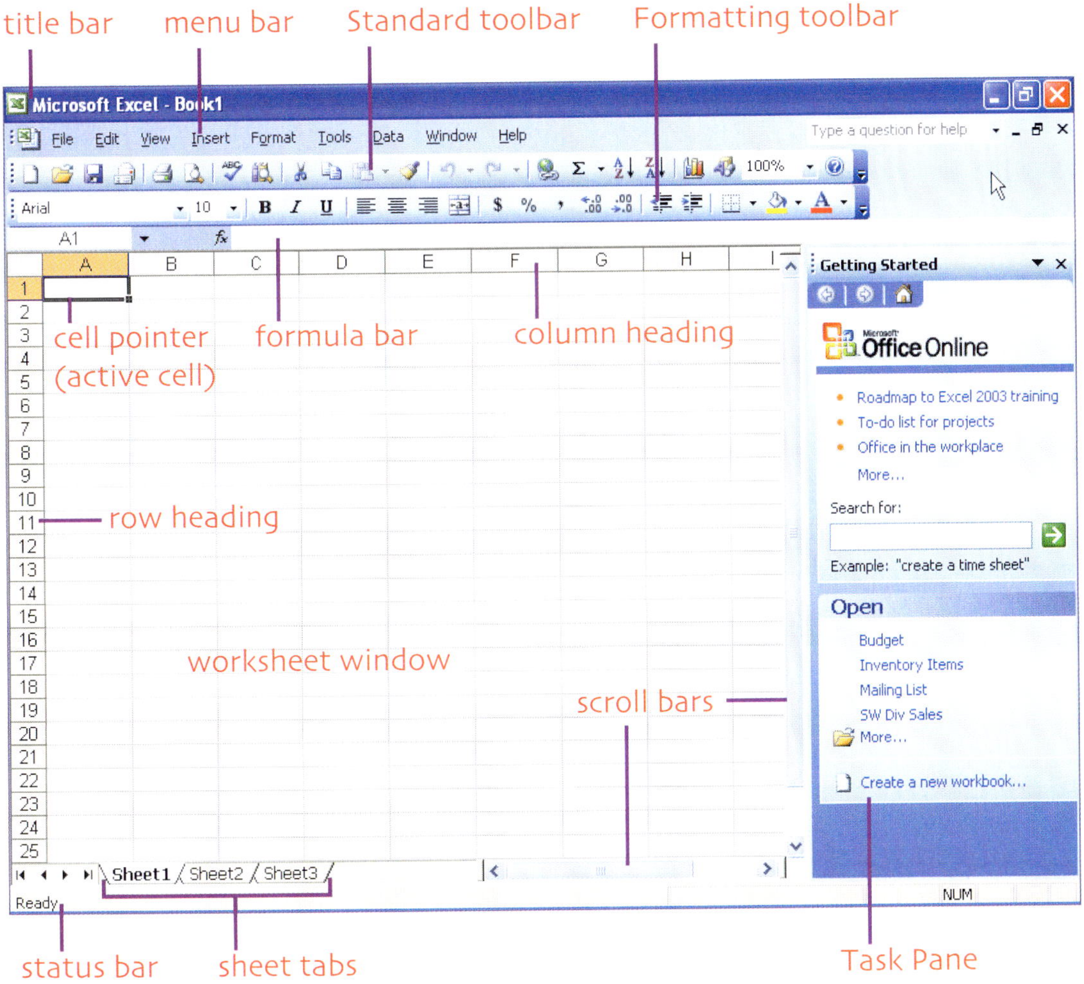
title bar
menu bar
Standard toolbar
Formatting toolbar
Microsoft Excel - Book1
File Edit View Insert Format Tools Data Window Help
Type a question for help
Arial
10
100%
A1
Getting Started
Office Online
Roadmap to Excel 2003 training
To-do list for projects
Office in the workplace
More...
Search for:
Example: "create a time sheet"
Open
Budget
Inventory Items
Mailing List
SW Div Sales
More...
Create a new workbook...
cell pointer (active cell)
formula bar
column heading
row heading
worksheet window
scroll bars
Sheet1
Sheet2
Sheet3
Ready
NUM
status bar
sheet tabs
Task Pane

look at excel (Mac OS)

Here are some of the important interface elements in Excel for Mac OS X.

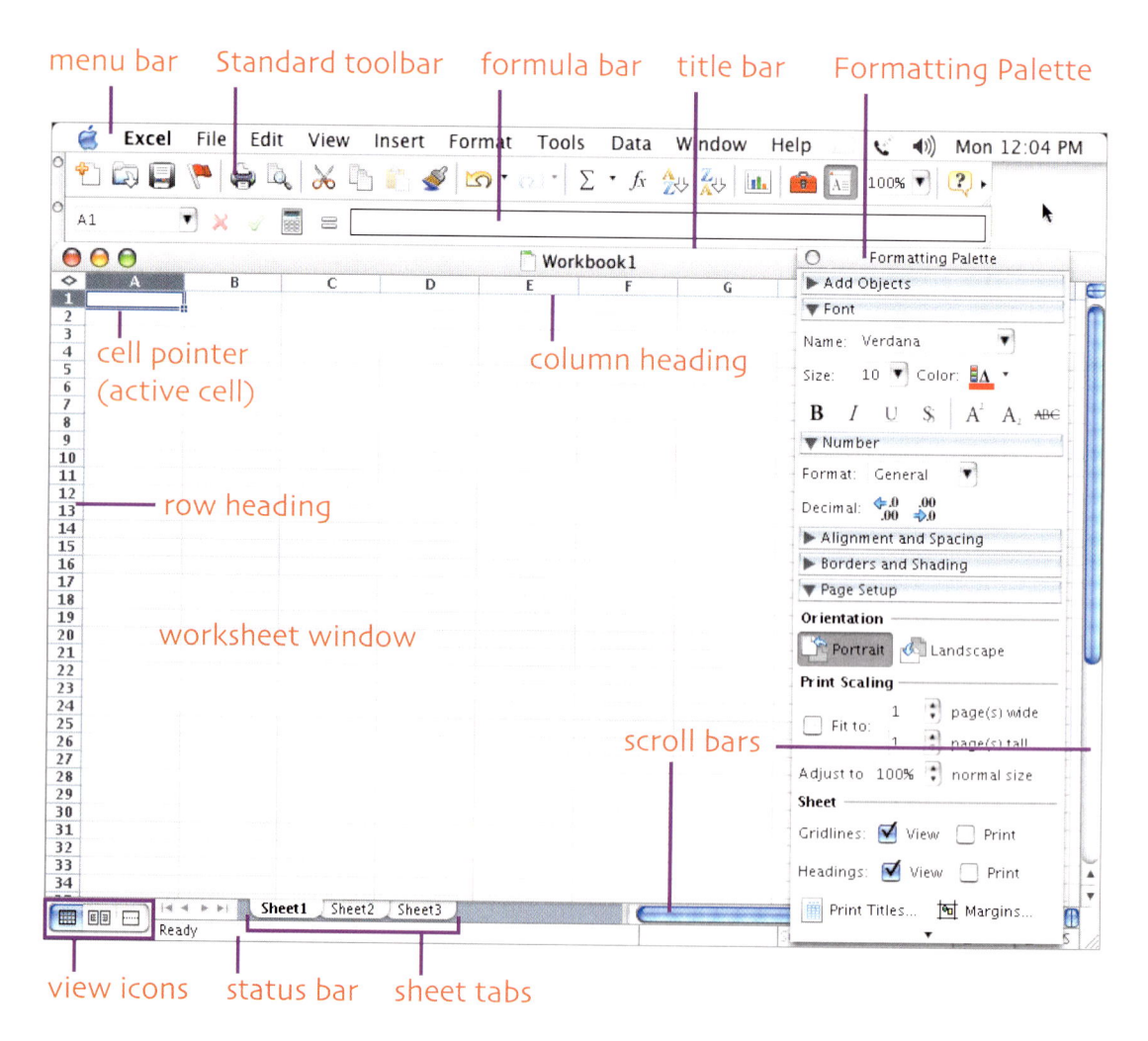

- menu bar
- Standard toolbar
- formula bar
- title bar
- Formatting Palette
- cell pointer (active cell)
- column heading
- row heading
- worksheet window
- scroll bars
- view icons
- status bar
- sheet tabs

meet microsoft excel

change the view

Excel for Windows has two views: Normal and Page Break Preview.

Excel for Mac OS has three views: Normal, Page Layout, and Page Break Preview.

You can change a window's view by choosing the name of the view you want from the View menu…

…or, in Excel 2004 for Macintosh, by clicking one of the View buttons at the bottom of the window. As shown here, you can point to a button to determine which view it's for.

Throughout this book, we'll stick to Normal view, which is illustrated on pages 5 and 6.

meet microsoft excel

scroll a window

Scroll bars on a window make it possible to shift window contents up or down (or sideways) to see hidden contents.

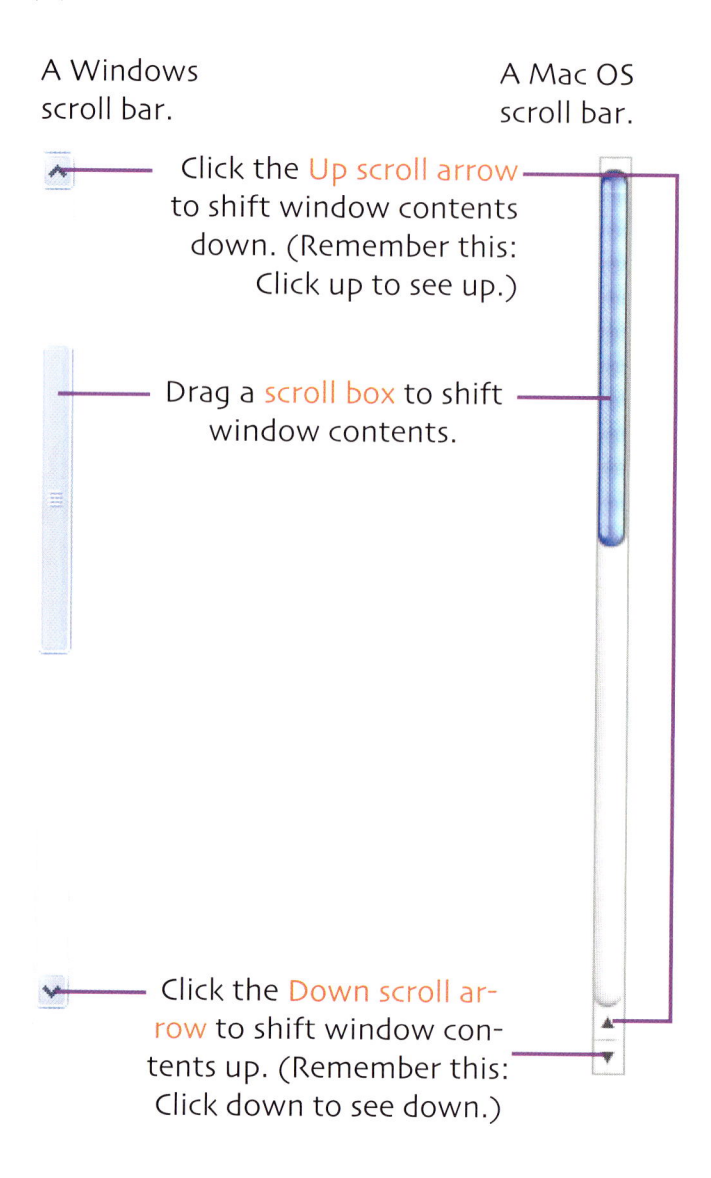

A Windows scroll bar.

A Mac OS scroll bar.

Click the Up scroll arrow to shift window contents down. (Remember this: Click up to see up.)

Drag a scroll box to shift window contents.

Click the Down scroll arrow to shift window contents up. (Remember this: Click down to see down.)

meet microsoft excel

choose from a menu

A menu is a list of commands that can be accessed from the menu bar at the top of the program window (Windows) or screen (Mac OS).

To display a menu, click its name.

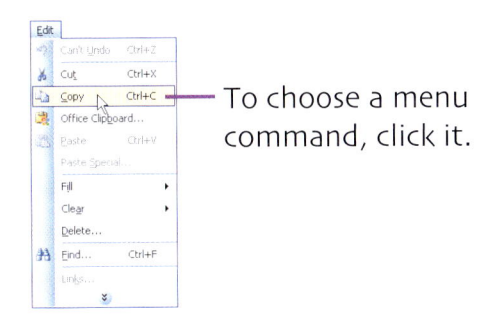

To choose a menu command, click it.

A submenu is a menu that pops out of another menu when you select it.

To choose a submenu command, display the submenu and click the command.

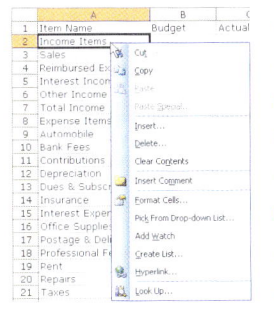

A contextual menu appears when you right-click something (Windows) or hold down the Control key while clicking something (Mac OS).

To choose a contextual menu command, display the menu and click the command.

meet microsoft excel 9

use a toolbar

Excel has a number of toolbars with buttons you can click to access commands quickly.

In Excel for Windows, two toolbars appear automatically: the Standard toolbar and the Formatting toolbar.

In Excel for Mac OS, one toolbar and a palette appear automatically: the Standard toolbar and the Formatting Palette.

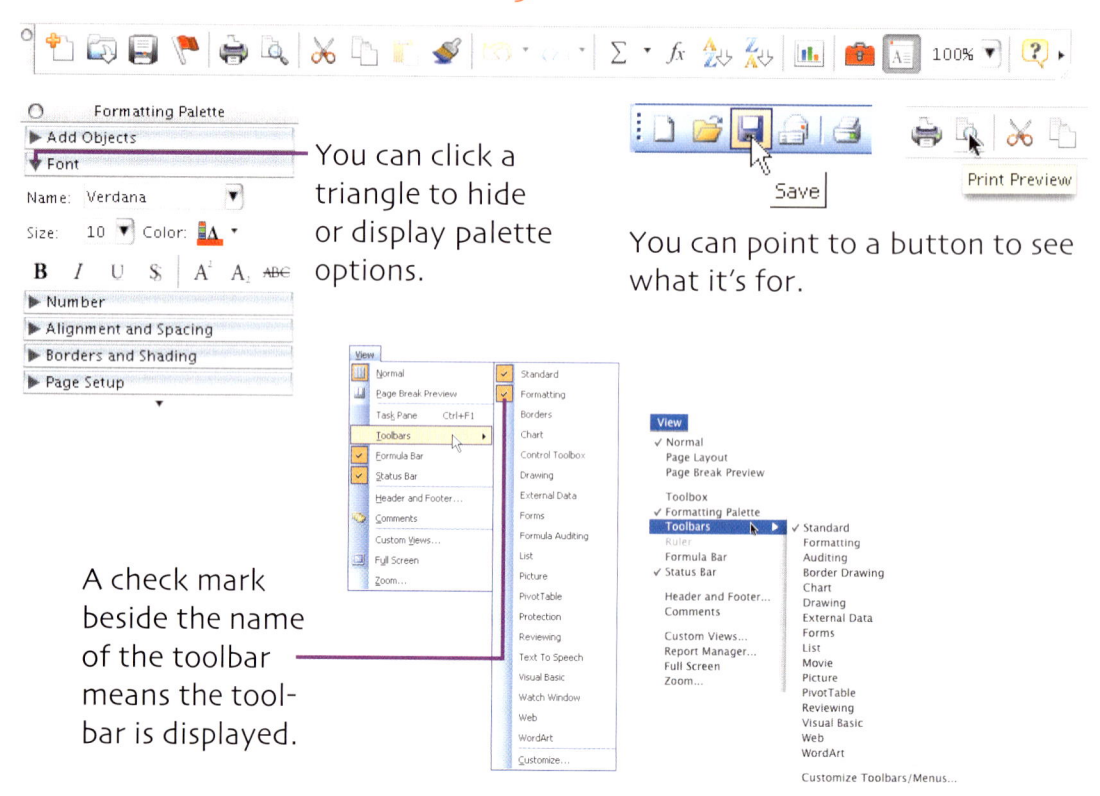

You can click a triangle to hide or display palette options.

You can point to a button to see what it's for.

A check mark beside the name of the toolbar means the toolbar is displayed.

To display a toolbar, choose its name from the Toolbars submenu under the View menu.

10   meet microsoft excel

have a dialog

A dialog (or dialog box) is a window that appears onscreen when your computer needs to communicate with you.

When a dialog offers options for you to complete a task, it can display the options in a number of ways.

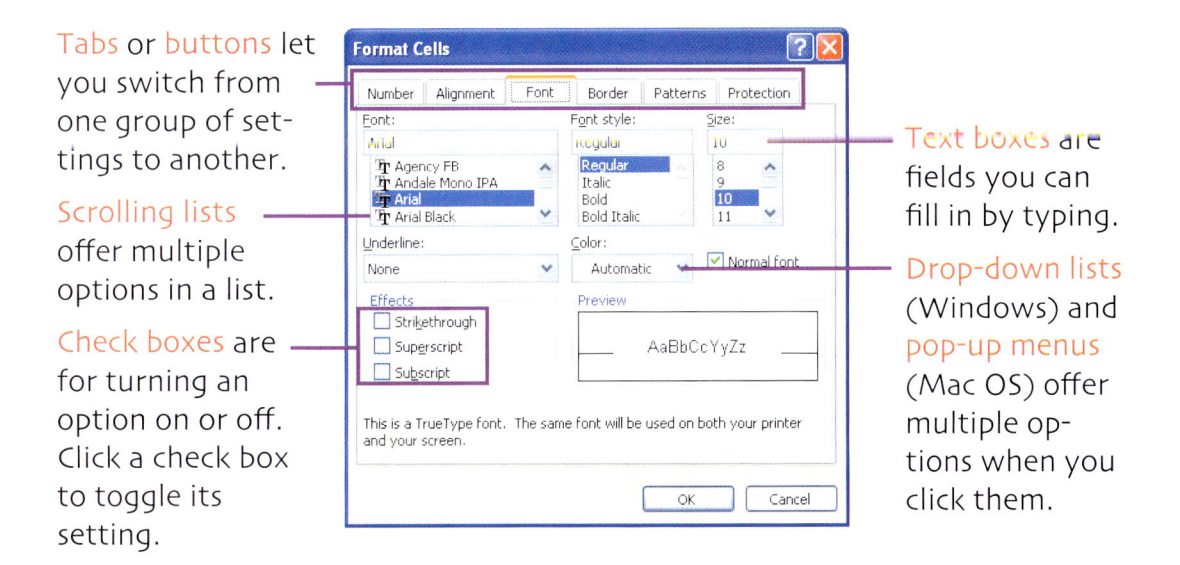

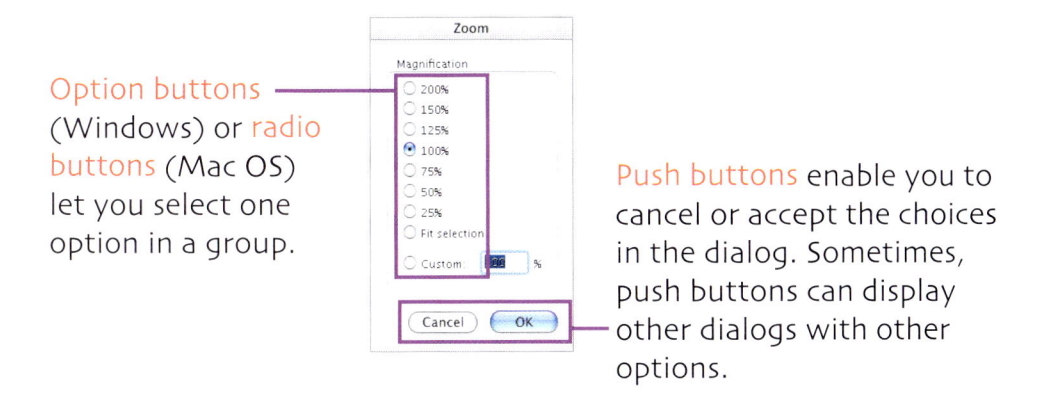

Tabs or buttons let you switch from one group of settings to another.

Scrolling lists offer multiple options in a list.

Check boxes are for turning an option on or off. Click a check box to toggle its setting.

Text boxes are fields you can fill in by typing.

Drop-down lists (Windows) and pop-up menus (Mac OS) offer multiple options when you click them.

Option buttons (Windows) or radio buttons (Mac OS) let you select one option in a group.

Push buttons enable you to cancel or accept the choices in the dialog. Sometimes, push buttons can display other dialogs with other options.

meet microsoft excel 11

exit or quit excel

When you're finished using Excel, you should exit or quit it.

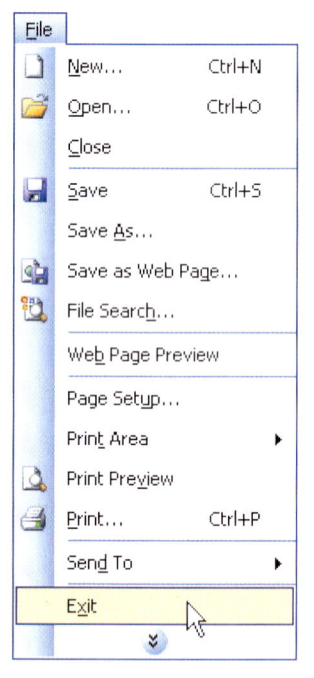

In Windows: Choose Exit from the File menu.

In Mac OS: Choose Quit Excel from the Excel menu.

If a document with unsaved changes is open, Excel displays a dialog that gives you a chance to save the document. (I tell you how to save documents in Chapter 2.)

extra bits

mouse around p. 3

- It is possible to get a multiple-button mouse for your Macintosh. But this book assumes you have a standard mouse with only one button.
- It's also possible to get a three-button mouse for your Windows PC. Frankly, I think two buttons are confusing enough, so I'll assume that's all your mouse has.
- You can also get a mouse with a roller—for Windows or Mac OS. (It's pretty common on Windows mice.) You can use the roller to scroll an active window. Since this feature doesn't work consistently, I don't bother talking about it in this book.

start or open excel p. 4

- These instructions assume you have installed the entire Microsoft Office suite of products, including Excel, Word, PowerPoint, and Outlook (or Entourage). If you have installed just Excel on your computer, consult the manual that came with it for instructions on how to start it.
- If you have a version of Excel other than Excel 2003 for Windows or Excel 2004 for Mac OS, you might have to follow a different procedure for starting Excel. Check the documentation that came with your version of Excel to learn how to start it.
- Chances are, your Start menu won't look exactly like mine. But if you follow the instructions, you should be able to find and start Excel using your Start menu.
- There are lots of ways to start Excel in Windows and Mac OS. If you have a method you prefer, go for it!

extra bits

look at excel (Mac OS) p. 6

- When you first launch Excel 2004 for Mac OS, it may display a worksheet window in Page Layout view. You can switch to Normal view shown here by clicking the Normal View icon at the bottom-left corner of the window. I tell you more about views on page 7.
- If the formula bar does not appear, choose Formula Bar from the View menu to display it.

scroll a window p. 8

- You can customize Mac OS X so the scroll arrows are at either end of the scroll bars. Choose System Preferences from the Apple menu and click the Appearance tab to get started.

choose from a menu p. 9

- Contextual menus are sometimes known as shortcut menus.
- If a menu command has a shortcut key, it appears on the menu beside the command. For example, the Save command has a shortcut key of Ctrl-S (in Windows) or Command-S (in Mac OS). Pressing that key combination invokes the Save command without displaying the File menu.

use a toolbar p. 10

- In Windows, the Standard and Formatting toolbars sometimes appear on the same line. If so, not all buttons may appear. You can display the toolbars on separate lines by dragging the move handle of either toolbar down until it appears on its own line.

have a dialog p. 11

- You can select any number of check boxes in a group, but you can select only one option or radio button in a group.

14 meet microsoft excel

2. create the workbook file

Excel documents are called workbook files. A workbook can include multiple sheets of information.

Excel supports two kinds of sheets for working with data:

• Worksheets, which are also known as spreadsheets, are for recording text and numerical information and performing calculations. Our project will use worksheets for the monthly budget information and the consolidation.

• Chart sheets are for displaying worksheet information as graphs or charts. Excel supports many types of charts, including the pie chart that's part of our project.

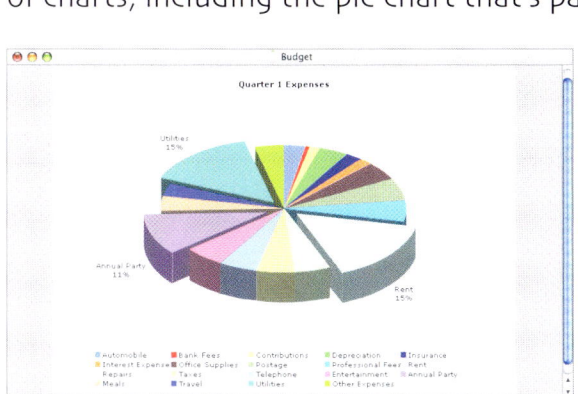

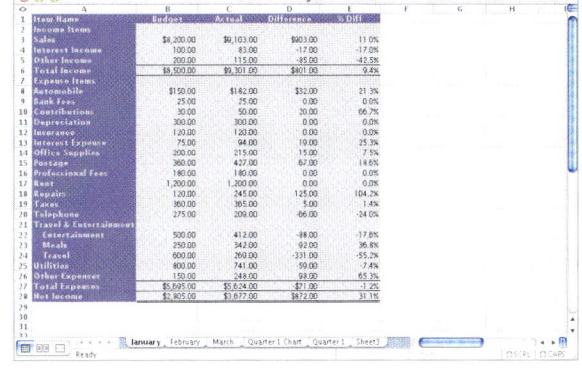

You can think of Excel sheets as pages in an Excel book—that's what I do. Then, when you create a workbook for a project—like our monthly budget with consolidation and chart—you can fill it with the sheets that apply to that project to keep everything together.

In this chapter, we'll create and save the workbook file we'll use to build our project.

15

create the workbook

Excel offers a number of ways to create a blank workbook file. The quickest and easiest way is with the New button.

1 Click the New button on the Standard toolbar.

Windows   Mac OS

A new workbook document appears. It displays a worksheet window, like the ones on pages 5 and 6.

2 In Mac OS, click the Normal View button at the bottom of the window to switch to Normal view.

16 create the workbook file

set view options (Windows)

You can set view options to determine which screen elements appear while you're working with Excel. It's a good idea to display the tools you'll need to complete this project before you start creating worksheets.

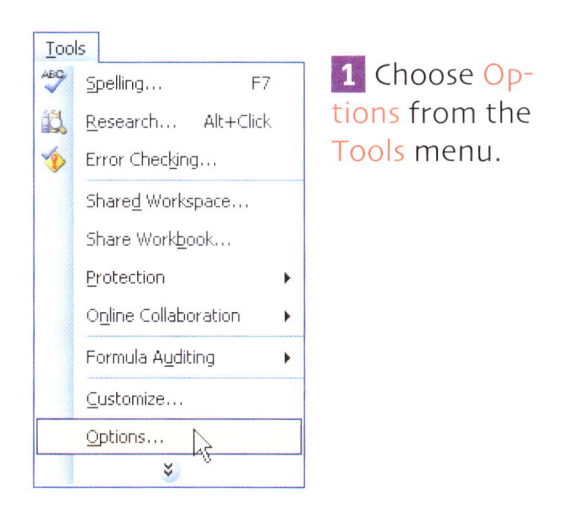

1 Choose Options from the Tools menu.

2 In the Options dialog that appears, click the View tab.

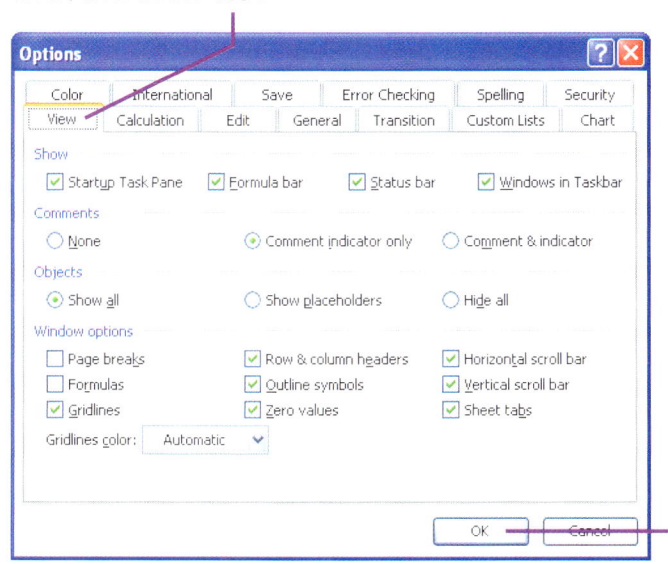

3 Make sure the following check boxes are turned on:

- Formula bar
- Gridlines
- Row & column headers
- Outline symbols
- Zero values
- Horizontal scroll bar
- Vertical scroll bar
- Sheet tabs

4 Click OK.

create the workbook file 17

set view prefs (Mac OS)

You can set view preferences to determine which screen elements appear while you're working with Excel. It's a good idea to display the tools you'll need to complete this project before you start creating worksheets.

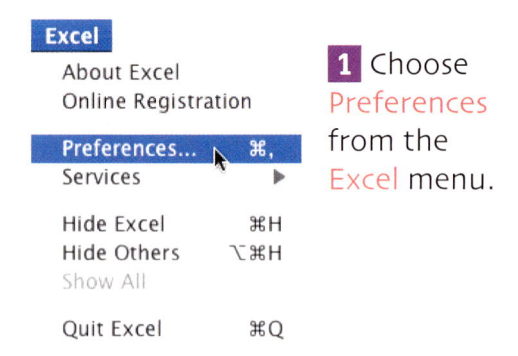

1 Choose Preferences from the Excel menu.

2 In the Preferences dialog that appears, click View.

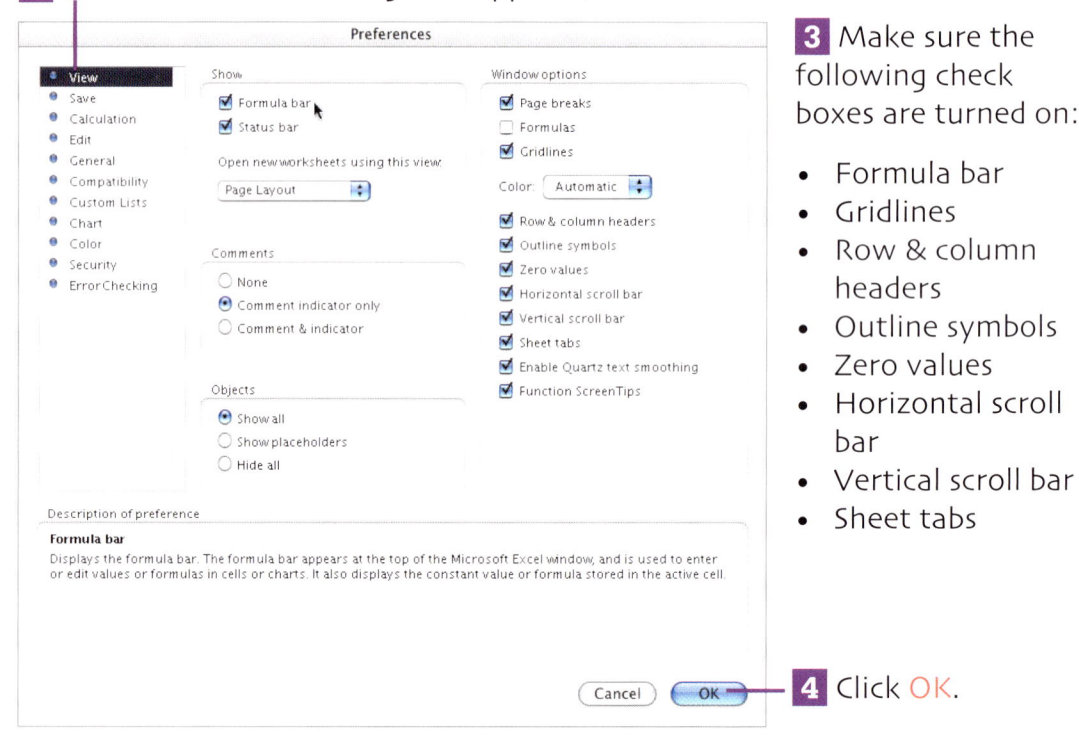

3 Make sure the following check boxes are turned on:

- Formula bar
- Gridlines
- Row & column headers
- Outline symbols
- Zero values
- Horizontal scroll bar
- Vertical scroll bar
- Sheet tabs

4 Click OK.

18   create the workbook file

save the workbook (Windows)

You can save a workbook file to keep a record of it on disk or to open and work with it at a later date. For this project, we'll save the workbook in the My Documents folder.

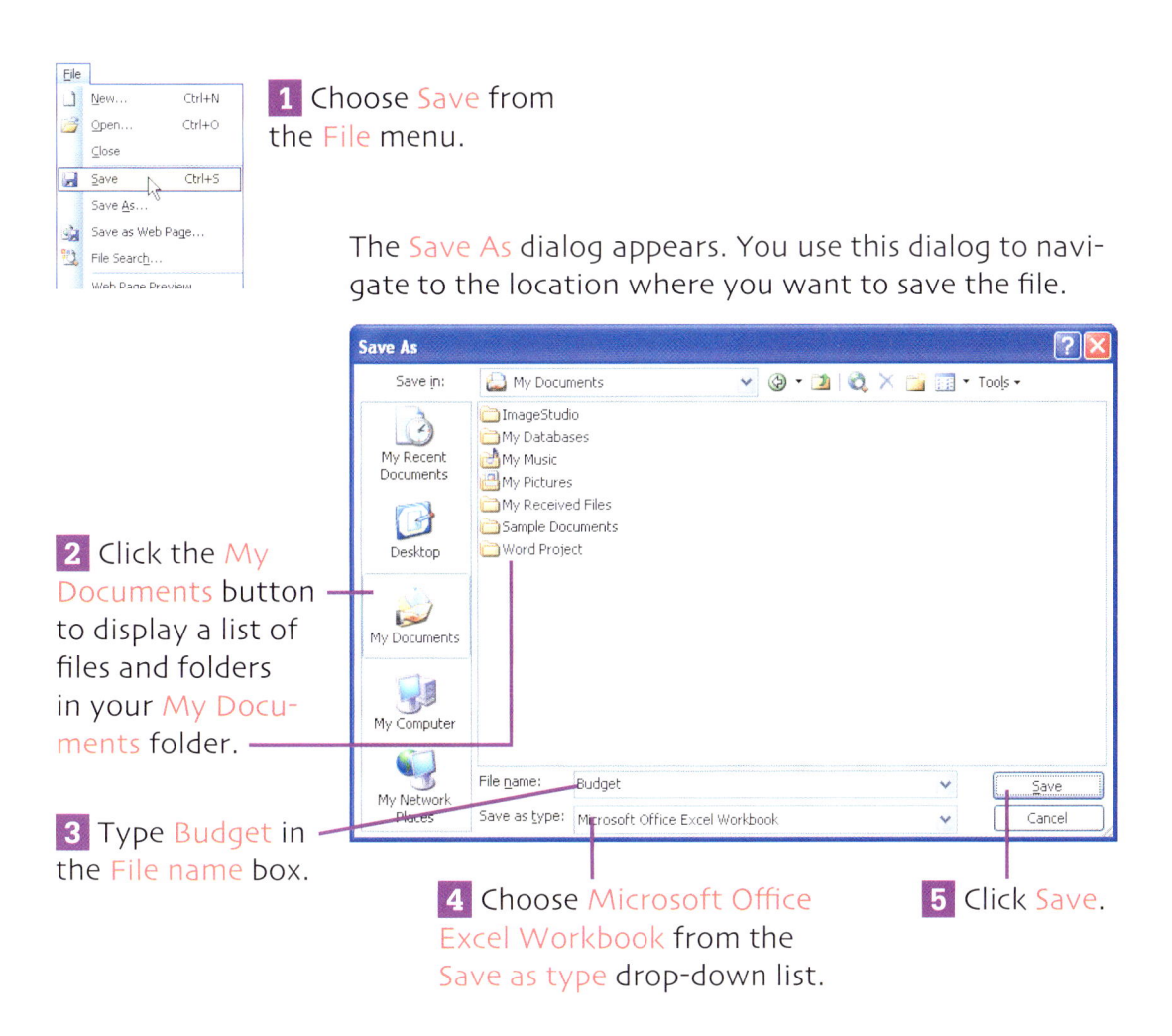

1 Choose Save from the File menu.

The Save As dialog appears. You use this dialog to navigate to the location where you want to save the file.

2 Click the My Documents button to display a list of files and folders in your My Documents folder.

3 Type Budget in the File name box.

4 Choose Microsoft Office Excel Workbook from the Save as type drop-down list.

5 Click Save.

The document is saved in your My Documents folder. Its name appears in the title bar.

create the workbook file 19

save the workbook (Mac OS)

You can save a document to keep a record of it on disk or to open and work with it at a later date. For this project, we'll save the workbook in the Documents folder inside your Home folder.

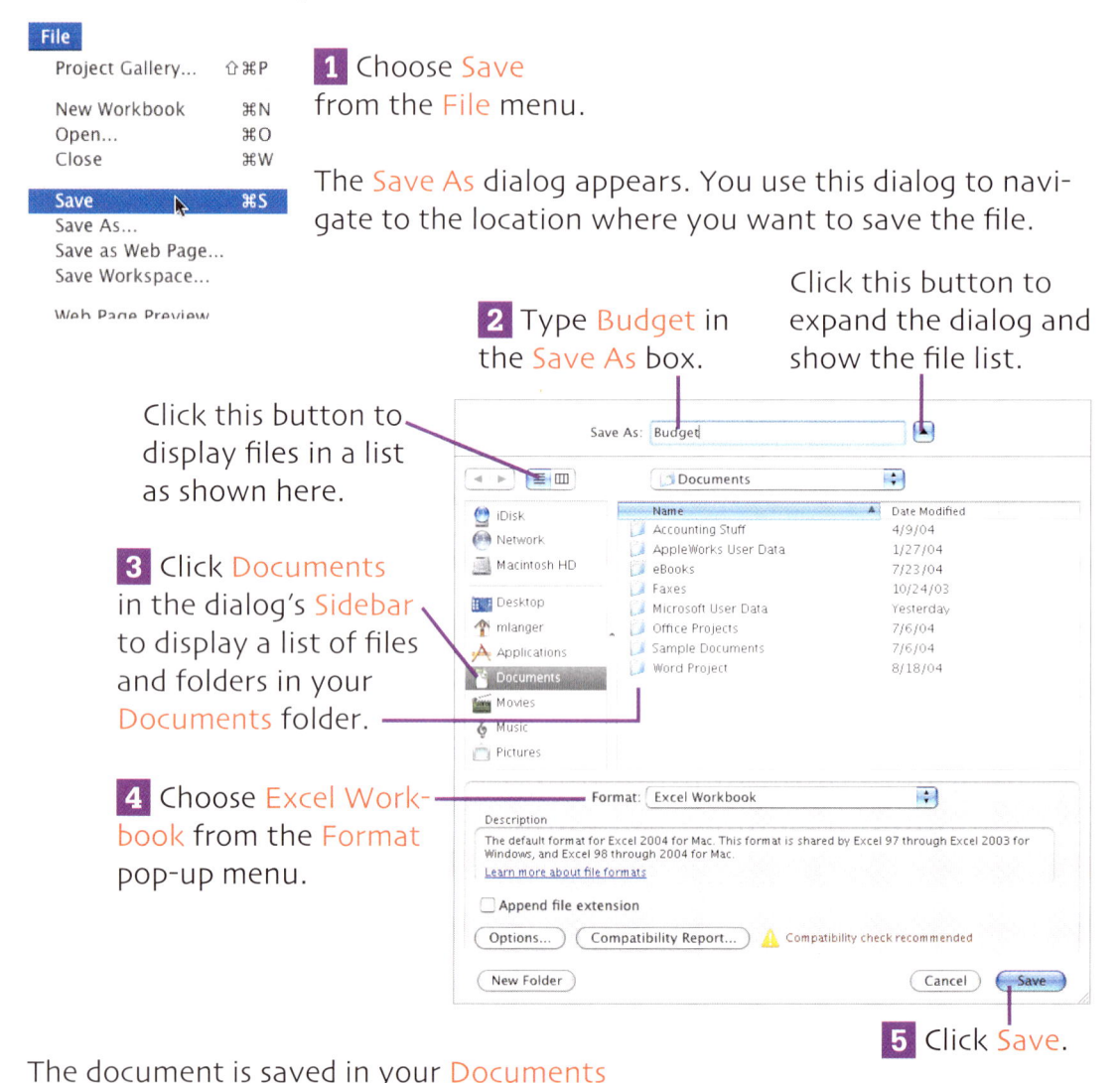

1 Choose Save from the File menu.

The Save As dialog appears. You use this dialog to navigate to the location where you want to save the file.

2 Type Budget in the Save As box.

Click this button to expand the dialog and show the file list.

Click this button to display files in a list as shown here.

3 Click Documents in the dialog's Sidebar to display a list of files and folders in your Documents folder.

4 Choose Excel Workbook from the Format pop-up menu.

5 Click Save.

The document is saved in your Documents folder. Its name appears in the title bar.

create the workbook file

extra bits

create the workbook p. 16

- In Mac OS, you can set preferences so new workbooks always appear in Normal view and the Formula bar appears automatically when you start Excel. Choose Preferences from the Excel menu and click View in the Preferences dialog that appears. In the Show area, turn on the Formula bar check box and choose Normal from the pop-up menu. Click OK to save your settings.

save the workbook pp. 19-20

- It's a good idea to save your workbook file occasionally as you build it. Just choose Save from the File menu or click the Save button on the Standard toolbar. Excel saves the current version of the file without displaying a dialog.

- To save a file with a different name or in a different disk location, choose Save As from the File menu. Then set options in the Save As dialog that appears to save the file. Remember that the original version of the file remains on disk but is not updated with any changes that you made since you saved it.

save the workbook (Mac OS) p. 20

- If you plan to share your workbook file with a Windows user, turn on the Append file extension check box in the Save As dialog. This adds the .xls file extension to the file so it is recognized by Windows as an Excel workbook file.

create the workbook file   **21**

3. build the budget worksheet

The primary element of our project is the monthly budget worksheet. This worksheet lists all of the income and expense categories with columns for budgeted amounts, actual amounts, dollar difference, and percent difference. It also includes subtotals and totals.

As you can see, an Excel worksheet window closely resembles an accountant's paper worksheet. It includes columns and rows that intersect at cells. To build our budget worksheet, we'll enter information into cells.

In this chapter, we'll create the budget worksheet as shown here. (We'll apply formatting to the worksheet so it looks more presentable later in this project.)

	A	B	C	D	E
1	Item Name	Budget	Actual	Difference	% Diff
2	Income Items				
3	Sales	8200	9103	903	0.11012195
4	Interest Income	100	83	-17	-0.17
5	Other Income	200	115	-85	-0.425
6	Total Income	8500	9301	801	0.09423529
7	Expense Items				
8	Automobile	150	182	32	0.21333333
9	Bank Fees	25	25	0	0
10	Contributions	30	50	20	0.66666667
11	Depreciation	300	300	0	0
12	Insurance	120	120	0	0
13	Interest Expense	75	94	19	0.25333333
14	Office Supplies	200	215	15	0.075
15	Postage	360	427	67	0.18611111
16	Professional Fees	180	180	0	0
17	Rent	1200	1200	0	0
18	Repairs	120	245	125	1.04166667
19	Taxes	360	365	5	0.01388889
20	Telephone	275	209	-66	-0.24
21	Travel & Entertainment				
22	Entertainment	500	412	-88	-0.176
23	Meals	250	342	92	0.368
24	Travel	600	269	-331	-0.5516667
25	Utilities	800	741	-59	-0.07375
26	Other Expenses	150	248	98	0.65333333
27	Total Expenses	5695	5624	-71	-0.0124671
28	Net Income	2805	3677	872	0.31087344

name the sheet

The sheet tabs at the bottom of the worksheet window enable you to identify the active sheet. Each new workbook file includes three worksheets named Sheet1, Sheet2, and Sheet3. You can change the name of a sheet to make it more descriptive.

It's easy to identify the active sheet. Its sheet tab is white and the sheet name appears in bold text. And, if you have sharp eyes, you may notice that the active sheet's tab seems to appear on top of the other tabs.

Windows

Mac OS

1 Double-click the Sheet1 sheet tab. The name of the tab becomes selected.

2 Type January. The text you type overwrites the selected sheet name.

3 Press Enter (Windows) or Return (Mac OS). The new name is saved.

build the budget worksheet

understand references

The concept of references or addressing is important when working with spreadsheets. A reference or address identifies the part of the worksheet that you are working with.

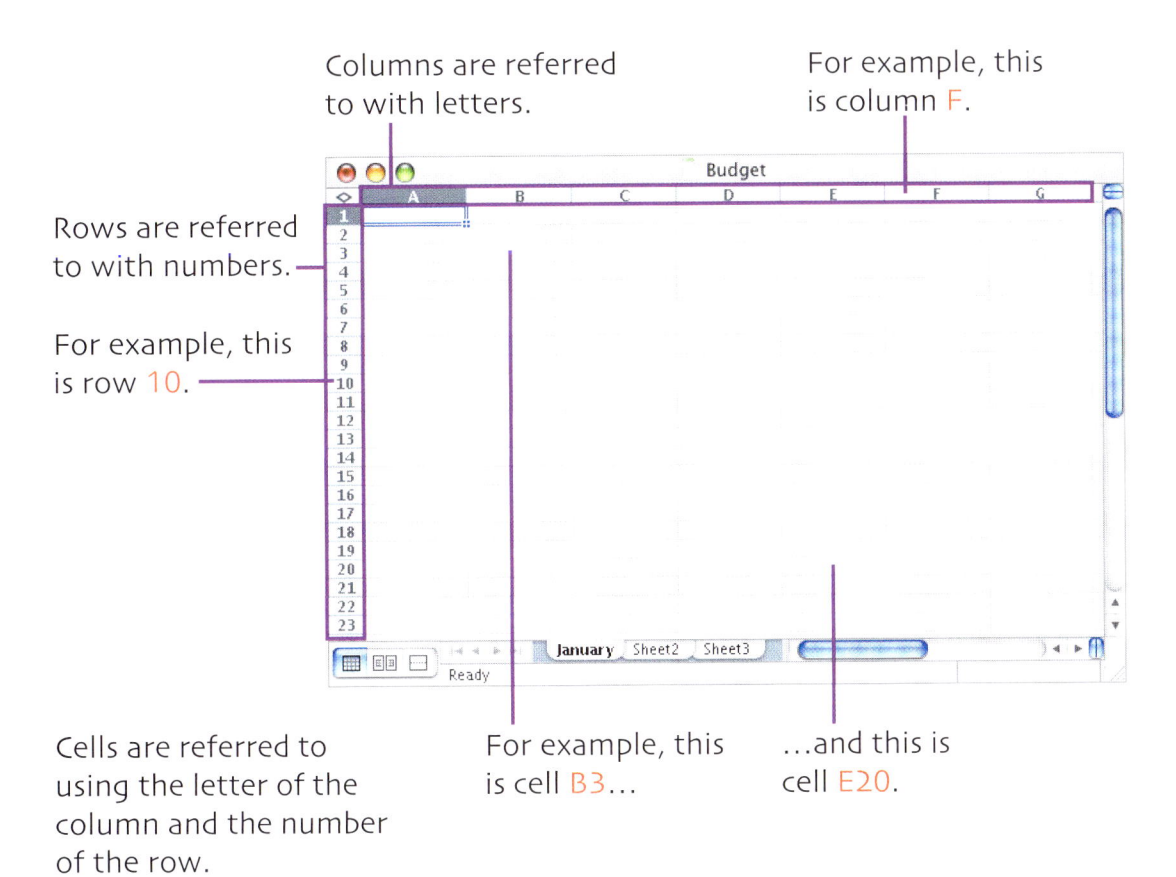

Columns are referred to with letters.

For example, this is column F.

Rows are referred to with numbers.

For example, this is row 10.

Cells are referred to using the letter of the column and the number of the row.

For example, this is cell B3...

...and this is cell E20.

build the budget worksheet   25

enter information

To build the budget worksheet, you'll enter three kinds of information into Excel worksheet cells:

• Labels (shown here in orange) are text entries that are used to identify information in the worksheet. For example, the word Budget is a label that will appear at the top of the column containing budget information.

• Values (shown here in green) are numbers, dates, or times. Values differ from labels in that you can perform mathematical calculations on them. In our budget worksheet, you'll enter numbers as values for budget and actual information.

	A	B	C	D	E
1	Item Name	Budget	Actual	Difference	% Diff
2	Income Items				
3	Sales	8200	9103	903	0.11012195
4	Interest Income	100	83	-17	-0.17
5	Other Income	200	115	-85	-0.425
6	Total Income	8500	9301	801	0.09423529
7	Expense Items				
8	Automobile	150	182	32	0.21333333
9	Bank Fees	25	25	0	0
10	Contributions	30	50	20	0.66666667
11	Depreciation	300	300	0	0
12	Insurance	120	120	0	0
13	Interest Expense	75	94	19	0.25333333
14	Office Supplies	200	215	15	0.075
15	Postage	360	427	67	0.18611111
16	Professional Fees	180	180	0	0
17	Rent	1200	1200	0	0
18	Repairs	120	245	125	1.04166667
19	Taxes	360	365	5	0.01388889
20	Telephone	275	209	-66	-0.24
21	Travel & Entertainment				
22	Entertainment	500	412	-88	-0.176
23	Meals	250	342	92	0.368
24	Travel	600	269	-331	-0.5516667
25	Utilities	800	741	-59	-0.07375
26	Other Expenses	150	248	98	0.65333333
27	Total Expenses	5695	5624	-71	-0.0124671
28	Net Income	2805	3677	872	0.31087344

• Formulas (shown here in yellow) are calculations written in a special notation that Excel can understand. When you enter a formula in a cell, Excel displays the result of the formula, not the formula itself. Formulas are a powerful feature of spreadsheet programs because they can perform all kinds of simple and complex calculations for you. In our budget worksheet, we'll use formulas to calculate the difference between budget and actual information in dollars and percents and to calculate column subtotals and totals.

build the budget worksheet

activate a cell

To enter information into a cell, you must activate it. That means moving the cell pointer to the cell in which you want to enter a label, value, or formula.

There are lots of ways to move the cell pointer, but rather than bombard you with a lot of unnecessary options, I'll tell you the two ways I use most.

Point and click:

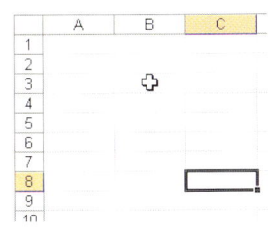

1 Move the mouse pointer, which looks like a cross, over the cell you want to activate.

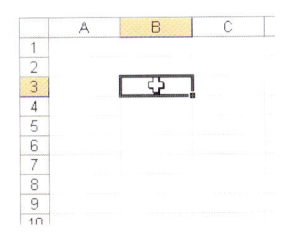

2 Press the mouse button once. The cell pointer moves to the cell you pointed to.

Use the arrow keys:

On the keyboard, press the arrow key corresponding to the direction you want the cell pointer to move.

For example, in this illustration, if I wanted to move the cell pointer from cell C8 to cell D6...

...I'd press the right arrow key once...   ...and the up arrow key twice.

build the budget worksheet

enter row headings

The row headings in our budget worksheet will identify the categories of income and expenses and label the subtotals and net income.

1 Activate cell A1 (the first cell in the worksheet).

2 Type Item Name.

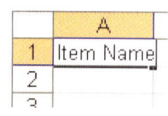

3 Press Enter (Windows) or Return (Mac OS). The cell pointer moves down one cell.

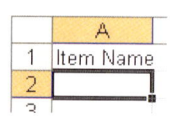

4 Repeat steps 2 and 3 for the following labels:

Income Items	Professional Fees
Sales	Rent
Interest Income	Repairs
Other Income	Taxes
Total Income	Telephone
Expense Items	Travel & Entertainment
Automobile	Entertainment
Bank Fees	Meals
Contributions	Travel
Depreciation	Utilities
Insurance	Other Expenses
Interest Expense	Total Expenses
Office Supplies	Net Income
Postage	

When you're finished, the worksheet should look like this.

28 **build the budget worksheet**

enter column headings

Our budget worksheet includes several columns of data and calculations. We'll use column headings to identify them.

1 Activate cell B1 (the one to the right of where you entered Item Name).

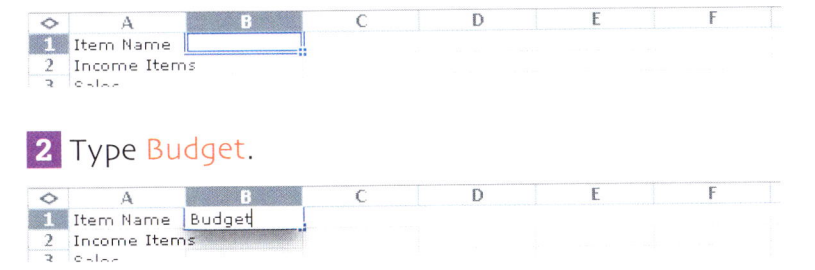

2 Type Budget.

3 Press Tab. The cell pointer moves one cell to the right.

4 Repeat steps 2 and 3 for the following labels:

Actual
Difference
% Diff

When you're finished, the worksheet should look like this.

build the budget worksheet 29

make a column wider

If the text in a cell has too many characters to fit in that cell, part of the cell's contents may appear truncated when you enter information in the cell to its right.

All the information you entered is still there; it's just hidden because the column it's in is too narrow. You can use Excel's AutoWidth feature to quickly make a column wider.

1 Position the mouse pointer on the right border of column **A**. The mouse pointer turns into a bar with two arrows coming out of it.

2 Double-click. The column automatically widens to accommodate the widest text in the column.

Have you been saving your work?

Now is a good time to click the **Save** button on the **Standard** toolbar to save your work up to this point.

30 **build the budget worksheet**

enter values

The whole purpose of the worksheet is to compare budgeted to actual amounts. It's time to enter those amounts. Since we need to enter values in two columns, we'll use an entry selection area.

1 Position the mouse pointer over cell B3.

2 Press the mouse button down and drag down and to the right to cell C26. All cells between B3 and C26 are enclosed in a selection box, but cell B3 remains the active cell.

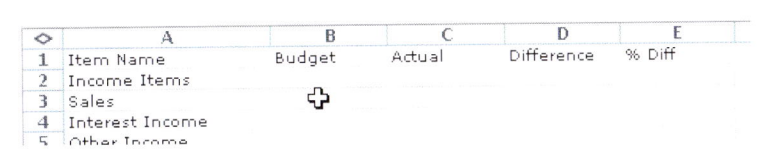

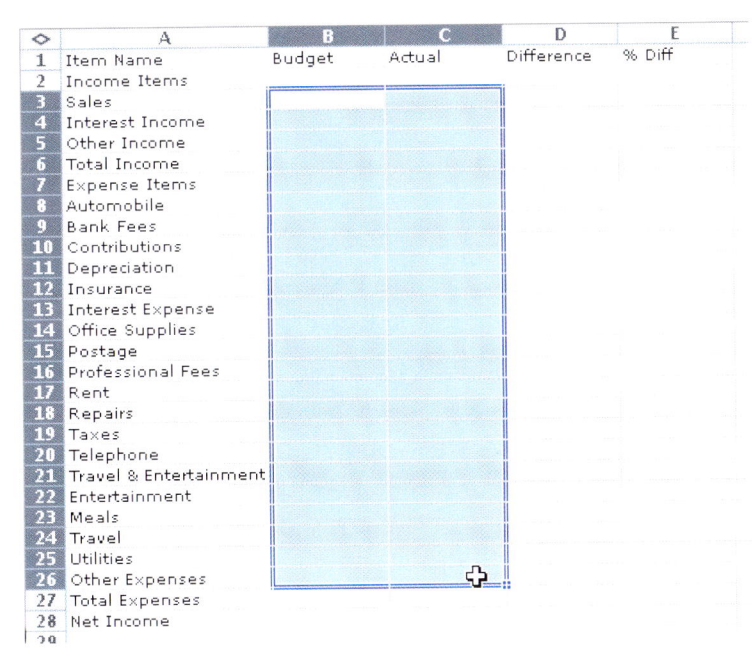

3 Type 8200. It appears in cell B3.

4 Press Enter (Windows) or Return (Mac OS). Cell B4 becomes the active cell.

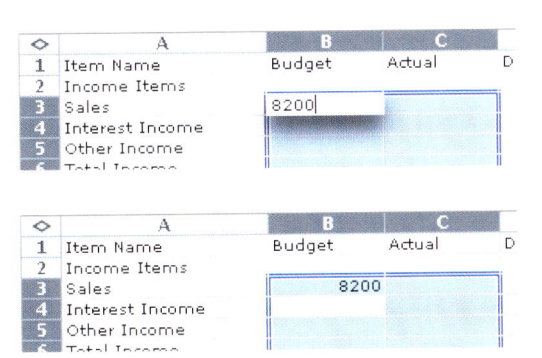

build the budget worksheet 31

enter values (cont'd)

5 Repeat steps 3 and 4 for the remaining values in column B shown here. When a cell that should remain blank becomes active, just press Enter or Return again to make the next cell active. After entering the last value in the column, when you press Enter or Return, cell C3 becomes active.

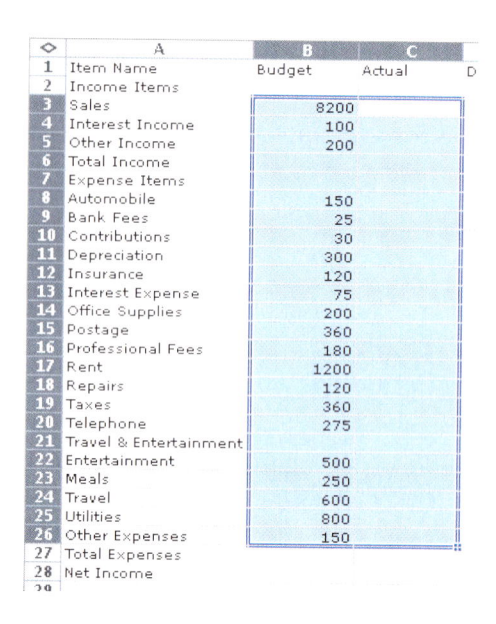

	A	B	C
1	Item Name	Budget	Actual
2	Income Items		
3	Sales	8200	
4	Interest Income	100	
5	Other Income	200	
6	Total Income		
7	Expense Items		
8	Automobile	150	
9	Bank Fees	25	
10	Contributions	30	
11	Depreciation	300	
12	Insurance	120	
13	Interest Expense	75	
14	Office Supplies	200	
15	Postage	360	
16	Professional Fees	180	
17	Rent	1200	
18	Repairs	120	
19	Taxes	360	
20	Telephone	275	
21	Travel & Entertainment		
22	Entertainment	500	
23	Meals	250	
24	Travel	600	
25	Utilities	800	
26	Other Expenses	150	
27	Total Expenses		
28	Net Income		

6 Repeat steps 3 and 4 for the values in column C shown here. When a cell that should remain blank becomes active, just press Enter or Return again to make the next cell active. After entering the last value in the column, when you press Return or Enter, cell B3 becomes active again.

	A	B	C
1	Item Name	Budget	Actual
2	Income Items		
3	Sales	8200	8103
4	Interest Income	100	83
5	Other Income	200	115
6	Total Income		
7	Expense Items		
8	Automobile	150	182
9	Bank Fees	25	25
10	Contributions	30	50
11	Depreciation	300	300
12	Insurance	120	120
13	Interest Expense	75	94
14	Office Supplies	200	215
15	Postage	360	427
16	Professional Fees	180	180
17	Rent	1200	1200
18	Repairs	120	245
19	Taxes	360	365
20	Telephone	275	209
21	Travel & Entertainment		
22	Entertainment	500	412
23	Meals	250	342
24	Travel	600	269
25	Utilities	800	741
26	Other Expenses	150	248
27	Total Expenses		
28	Net Income		

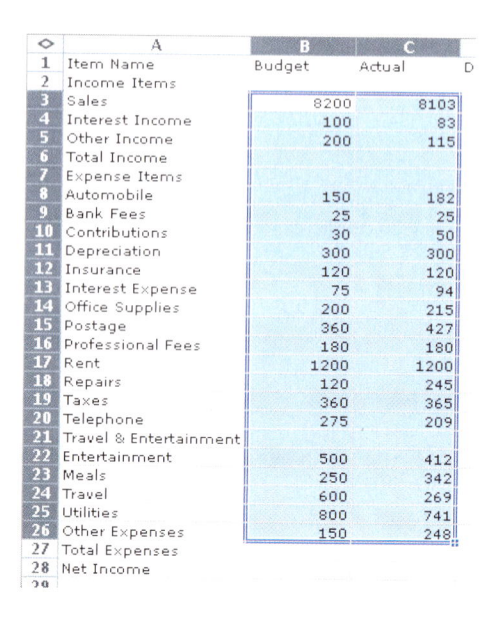

7 Click anywhere in the worksheet window to deselect the selected cells.

build the budget worksheet

calculate a difference

Column D, which will display the difference between budgeted and actual amounts, will contain simple formulas that subtract one cell's contents from another's using cell references. In this step, we'll write the first formula. Later, we'll copy the formula to other cells in the column.

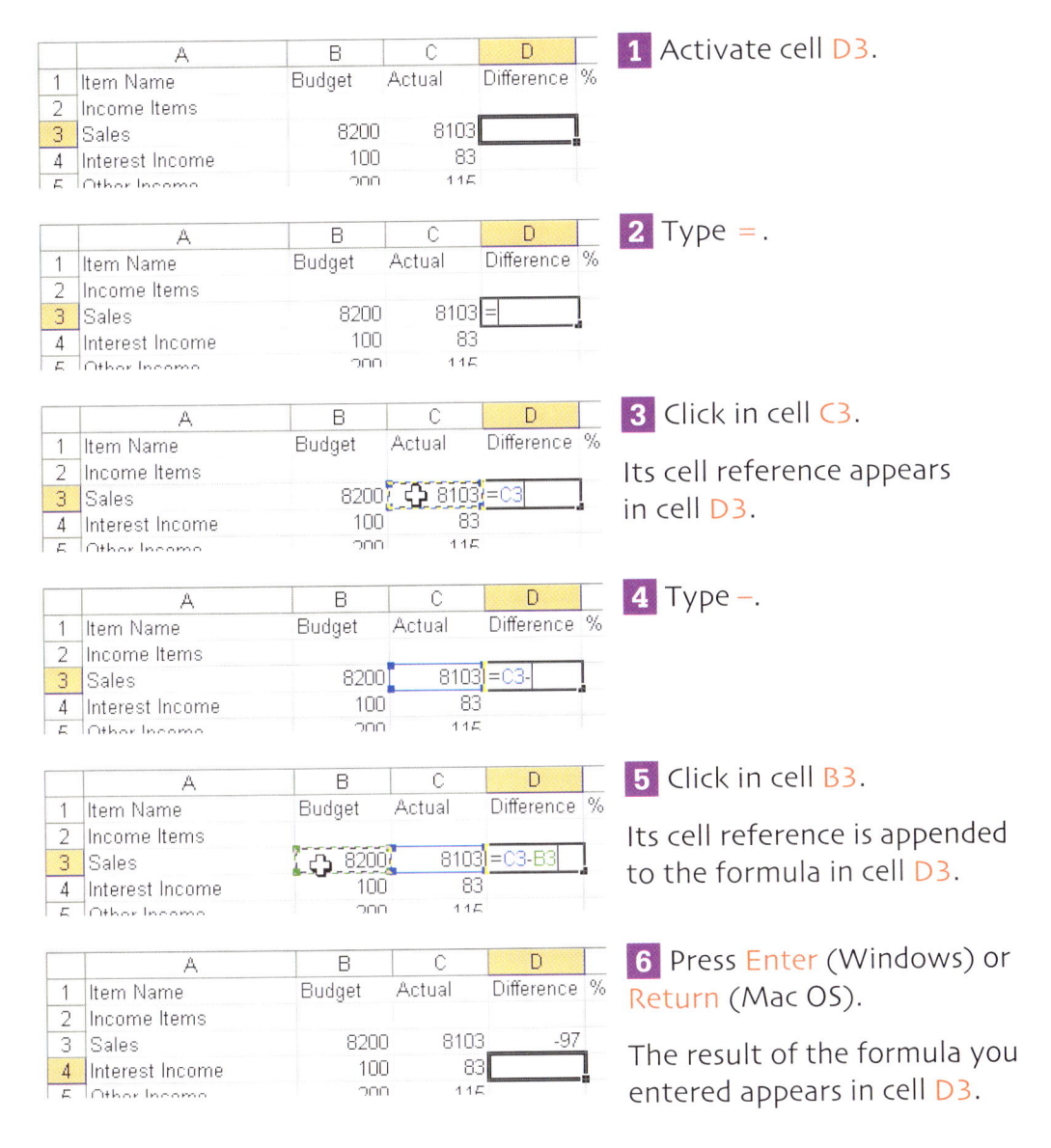

1 Activate cell D3.

2 Type =.

3 Click in cell C3.

Its cell reference appears in cell D3.

4 Type –.

5 Click in cell B3.

Its cell reference is appended to the formula in cell D3.

6 Press Enter (Windows) or Return (Mac OS).

The result of the formula you entered appears in cell D3.

build the budget worksheet 33

calculate a percent diff

Column E calculates the percent difference between the budgeted and actual amounts. The percentage is based on the budgeted amount. We'll write the first formula now and copy it to other cells in column E later.

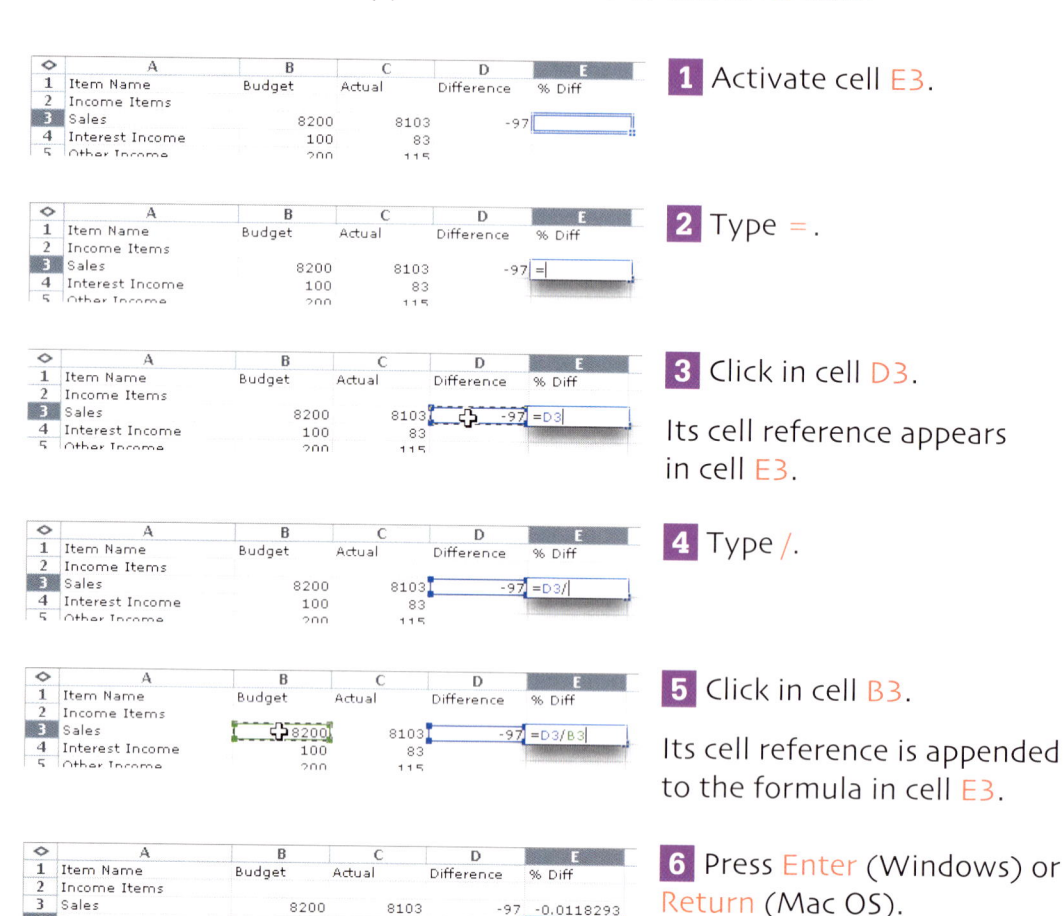

1 Activate cell E3.

2 Type =.

3 Click in cell D3.

Its cell reference appears in cell E3.

4 Type /.

5 Click in cell B3.

Its cell reference is appended to the formula in cell E3.

6 Press Enter (Windows) or Return (Mac OS).

The result of the formula you entered appears in cell E3.

build the budget worksheet

sum some values

Although you can write a formula that adds multiple cell references, one cell at a time, it's much easier to use Excel's SUM function to add up the contents of a range of cells. Here are two ways to enter the SUM function in formulas to create subtotals for the values in column B.

Use the AutoSum button:

1 Activate cell B6.

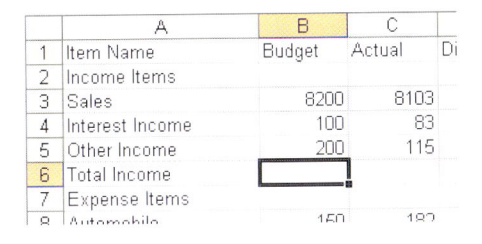

2 Click the AutoSum button on the Standard toolbar.

Excel writes a formula that uses the SUM function to add a range of cells. A colored box appears around the cells included in the formula.

A function tooltip may appear as you enter the formula.

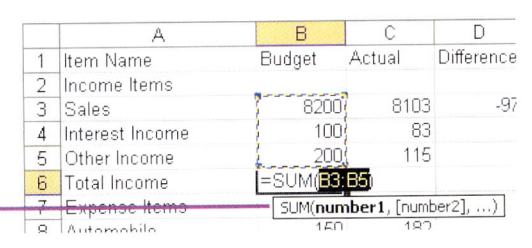

3 If the formula is correct (as shown here), press Enter (Windows) or Return (Mac OS).

If the formula is not correct, enter the correct range reference and press Enter (Windows) or Return (Mac OS).

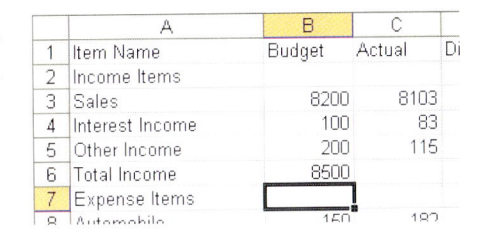

The result of the formula appears in cell B6.

build the budget worksheet 35

sum some values (cont'd)

Type and drag:

1 Activate cell B27.

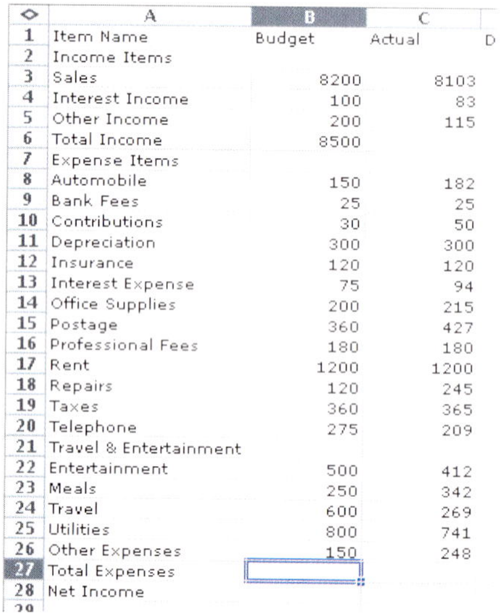

2 Type =SUM(.

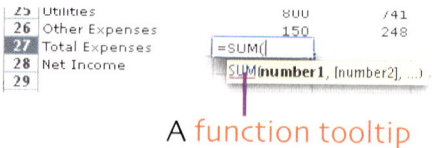

A function tooltip may appear as you enter the formula.

3 Position the mouse pointer on cell B8.

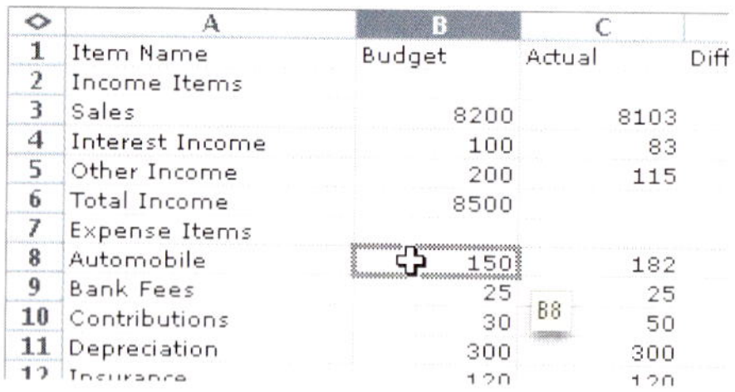

4 Press the mouse button and drag down to cell B26. All cells you dragged over are selected and referenced in the formula in cell B27.

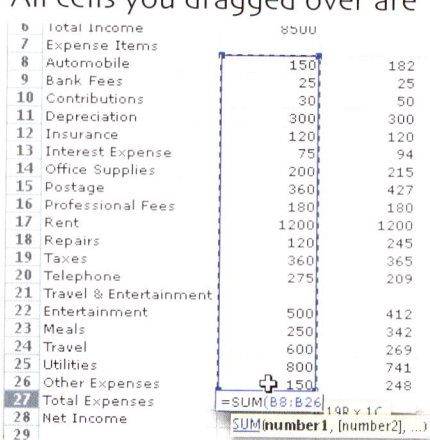

5 Type).

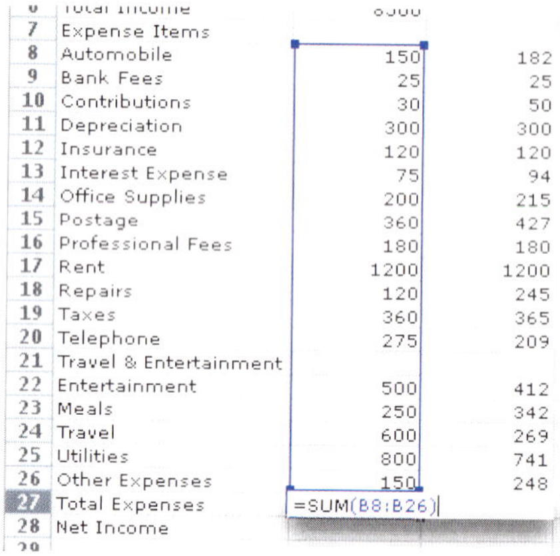

6 Press Enter (Windows) or Return (Mac OS). The result of the formula appears in cell B27.

36 build the budget worksheet

calculate net income

The final row of the worksheet contains cells to calculate the net income: total income minus total expenses. Here's how to enter that final formula.

1 Activate cell B28.

2 Type =.

3 Click cell B6. Its reference appears in the formula in cell B28.

4 Type −.

5 Click cell B27. Its reference appears in the formula in cell B28.

6 Press Enter (Windows) or Return (Mac OS). The result of the formula appears in cell B28.

Have you been saving your work?

Now is a good time to click the Save button on the Standard toolbar to save your work up to this point.

build the budget worksheet 37

copy formulas

Excel lets you copy a formula in one cell to another cell that needs a similar formula. This can save a lot of time when building a worksheet with multiple columns or rows that need similar formulas.

For example, you can copy the formula in cell B6 (total income for budgeted amounts) to cell C6 (total income for actual amounts).

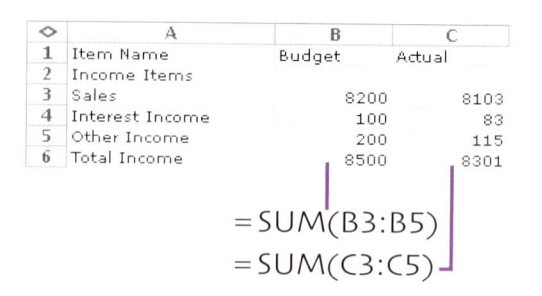

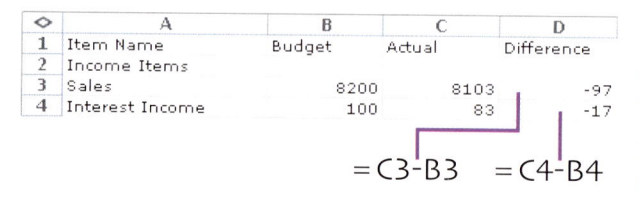

=SUM(B3:B5)
=SUM(C3:C5)

Similarly, you can copy the formula in cell D3 (difference between budgeted and actual sales) to D4 (difference between budgeted and actual interest income).

=C3-B3   =C4-B4

Excel automatically rewrites the cell references so they refer to the correct cells. You can view a cell's formula by activating the cell and looking in the formula bar near the top of the window.

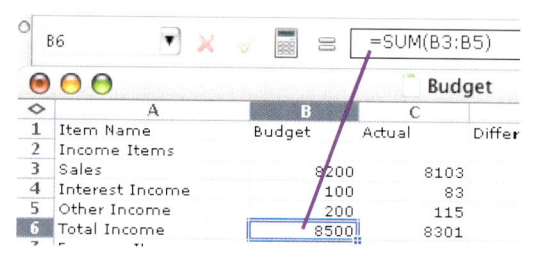

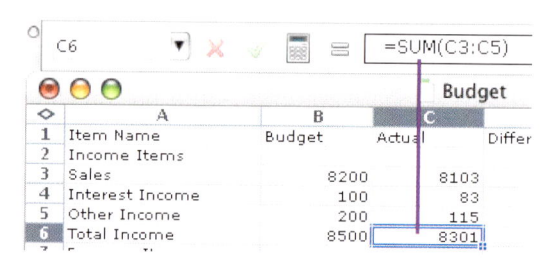

38   **build the budget worksheet**

copy and paste

One way to copy formulas is with the Copy and Paste commands.

1 Drag to select cells D3 and E3.

2 Choose Copy from the Edit menu.

A marquee appears around selected cells.

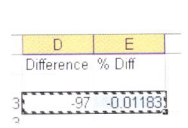

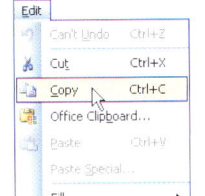

3 Activate cell D8.

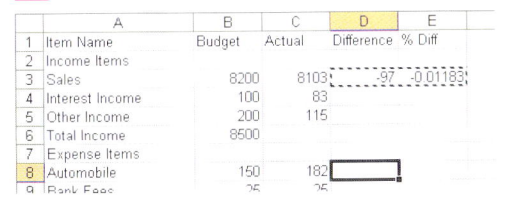

4 Choose Paste from the Edit menu.

The formulas in cells D3 and E3 are copied to cells D8 and E8. The marquee remains around the originally selected cells, indicating that they can be pasted elsewhere.

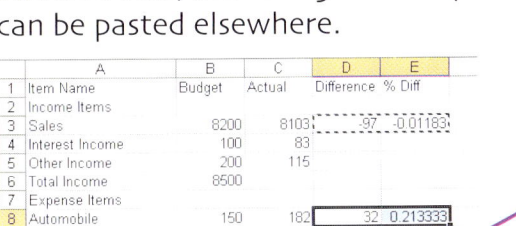

5 Activate cell D22.

6 Press Enter. The formulas are copied to cells D22 and E22. The marquee disappears, indicating the selection can no longer be pasted elsewhere.

Paste Options button (see extra bits)

build the budget worksheet

use the fill handle

A quick way to copy the contents of one cell to one or more adjacent cells is with the fill handle. We'll use the fill handle to finish up the worksheet entries.

1 Activate cell B6.

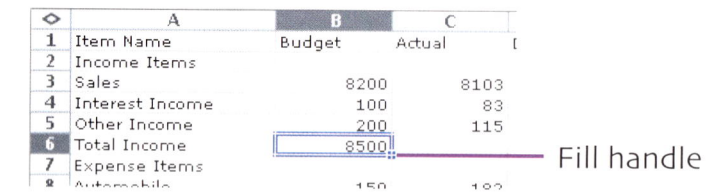

— Fill handle

2 Position the mouse pointer on the selection's fill handle—a tiny square in the bottom-right corner of the selection box. The mouse pointer turns into a black cross.

3 Press the mouse button and drag to the right. As you drag, the mouse pointer may change and a black or gray border stretches over the cells you pass over.

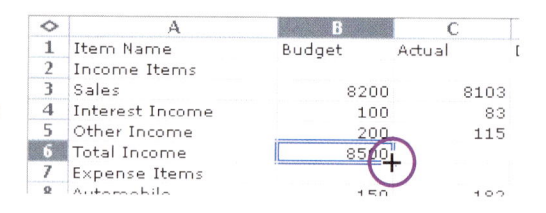

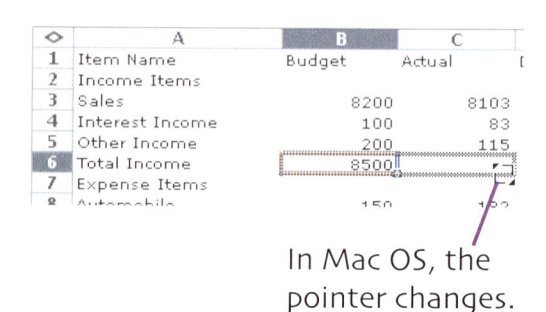

In Mac OS, the pointer changes.

4 When the border surrounds cells B6 and C6, release the mouse button. The formula in cell B6 is copied to cell C6.

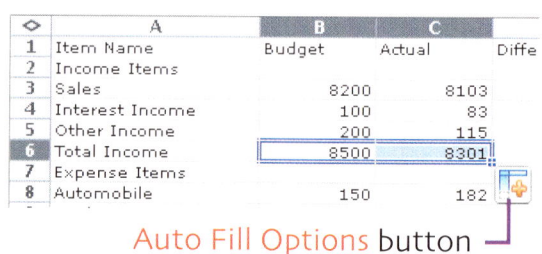

Auto Fill Options button (see extra bits)

40 **build the budget worksheet**

5 Repeat steps 1–4 for cell B27 to copy its formula to C27 and for cell B28 to copy its formula to cell C28. When you're finished, the worksheet should look like this.

6 Drag to select cells D3 and E3.

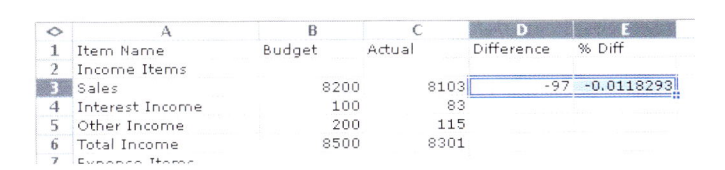

7 Position the mouse pointer on the selection's fill handle.

8 Press the mouse button down and drag so the border completely surrounds cells D3 through E6.

9 Release the mouse button. The two formulas are copied down to the cells you dragged over.

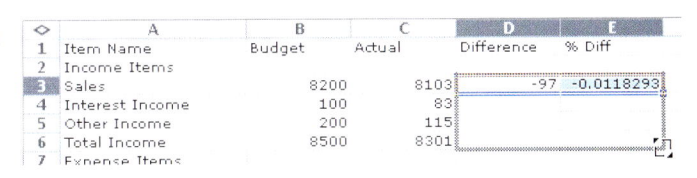

build the budget worksheet   **41**

use the fill handle (cont'd)

10 Repeat steps 6–9 to copy cells D8 and E8 to the range beneath it (shown here) and cells D22 and E22 to the range beneath it.

	A	B	C	D	E
1	Item Name	Budget	Actual	Difference	% Diff
2	Income Items				
3	Sales	8200	9103	903	0.11012195
4	Interest Income	100	83	-17	-0.17
5	Other Income	200	115	-85	-0.425
6	Total Income	8500	9301	801	0.09423529
7	Expense Items				
8	Automobile		150	182	32	0.21333333
9	Bank Fees	25	25		
10	Contributions	30	50		
11	Depreciation	300	300		
12	Insurance	120	120		
13	Interest Expense	75	94		
14	Office Supplies	200	215		
15	Postage	360	427		
16	Professional Fees	180	180		
17	Rent	1200	1200		
18	Repairs	120	245		
19	Taxes	360	365		
20	Telephone	275	209		
21	Travel & Entertainment				

When you're finished, the worksheet should look like this.

	A	B	C	D	E
1	Item Name	Budget	Actual	Difference	% Diff
2	Income Items				
3	Sales	8200	9103	903	0.11012195
4	Interest Income	100	83	-17	-0.17
5	Other Income	200	115	-85	-0.425
6	Total Income	8500	9301	801	0.09423529
7	Expense Items				
8	Automobile	150	182	32	0.21333333
9	Bank Fees	25	25	0	0
10	Contributions	30	50	20	0.66666667
11	Depreciation	300	300	0	0
12	Insurance	120	120	0	0
13	Interest Expense	75	94	19	0.25333333
14	Office Supplies	200	215	15	0.075
15	Postage	360	427	67	0.18611111
16	Professional Fees	180	180	0	0
17	Rent	1200	1200	0	0
18	Repairs	120	245	125	1.04166667
19	Taxes	360	365	5	0.01388889
20	Telephone	275	209	-66	-0.24
21	Travel & Entertainment				
22	Entertainment	500	412	-88	-0.176
23	Meals	250	342	92	0.368
24	Travel	600	269	-331	-0.5516667
25	Utilities	800	741	-59	-0.07375
26	Other Expenses	150	248	98	0.65333333
27	Total Expenses	5420	5415	-5	-0.0009225
28	Net Income	3080	2886	-194	-0.062987

Have you been saving your work?

Now is a good time to click the Save button on the Standard toolbar to save your work up to this point.

42 build the budget worksheet

change a value

In reviewing this worksheet, I realize that we made an error when entering values. The actual sales amount for the month wasn't 8103 as we entered. It was really 9103! Better enter the correct value now.

1 Activate cell C3.

	A	B	C	D	E
1	Item Name	Budget	Actual	Difference	% Diff
2	Income Items				
3	Sales	8200	8103	-97	-0.01183
4	Interest Income	100	83	-17	-0.17
5	Other Income	200	115	85	0.425

2 Type 9103. This new value overwrites the value already entered.

	A	B	C	D	E
1	Item Name	Budget	Actual	Difference	% Diff
2	Income Items				
3	Sales	8200	9103	-97	-0.01183
4	Interest Income	100	83	-17	-0.17
5	Other Income	200	115	85	0.425

3 Press Enter (Windows) or Return (Mac OS).

The value changes, but what's more important is that all of the formulas that referenced that value, either directly or indirectly, also change. Compare the orange highlighted cells in this illustration with the same cells in the illustration on the previous page to see for yourself.

This is the reason we use spreadsheet programs!

	A	B	C	D	E
1	Item Name	Budget	Actual	Difference	% Diff
2	Income Items				
3	Sales	8200	9103	903	0.110122
4	Interest Income	100	83	-17	-0.17
5	Other Income	200	115	-85	-0.425
6	Total Income	8500	9301	801	0.094235
7	Expense Items				
8	Automobile	150	182	32	0.213333
9	Bank Fees	25	25	0	0
10	Contributions	30	50	20	0.666667
11	Depreciation	300	300	0	0
12	Insurance	120	120	0	0
13	Interest Expense	75	94	19	0.253333
14	Office Supplies	200	215	15	0.075
15	Postage	360	427	67	0.186111
16	Professional Fees	180	180	0	0
17	Rent	1200	1200	0	0
18	Repairs	120	245	125	1.041667
19	Taxes	360	365	5	0.013889
20	Telephone	275	209	-66	-0.24
21	Travel & Entertainment				
22	Entertainment	500	412	-88	-0.176
23	Meals	250	342	92	0.368
24	Travel	600	269	-331	-0.55167
25	Utilities	800	741	-59	-0.07375
26	Other Expenses	150	248	98	0.653333
27	Total Expenses	5695	5624	-71	-0.01247
28	Net Income	2805	3677	872	0.310873

build the budget worksheet

extra bits

name the sheet p. 24

- As you'll see in Chapter 8, you can instruct Excel to automatically display a sheet name in a printed report's header or footer. That's a good reason to give a sheet an appropriate name.

activate a cell p. 27

- When you use the point-and-click method for activating a cell, you must click. If you don't click, the cell pointer won't move and the cell you're pointing to won't be activated.

enter row headings p. 28

- When you enter text in a cell, Excel's AutoComplete feature may suggest entries based on previous entries in the column.

13	Interest Expense
14	Office Supplies
15	Postage
16	Postage
17	

  To accept an entry, press Enter (Windows) or Return (Mac OS) when it appears. Otherwise, just keep typing what you want to enter. The AutoComplete suggestion will eventually go away.

make a column wider p. 30

- You can't change the width of a single cell. You must change the width of the entire column the cell is in.

enter values pp. 31–32

- You can enter any values you like in this step. But if you enter the same values I do, you can later compare the results of your formulas to mine to make sure the formulas you enter in the next step are correct.

- Do not include currency symbols or commas when entering values. Doing so will apply number formatting. I explain how to format cell contents, including values, in Chapter 6.

- If you use the arrow keys to move from one cell to the next, the selection area disappears. Although you can enter values without a selection area, using a selection area makes it easier to move from one cell to another.

- If, after entering values, you discover that one of the values is incorrect, activate the cell with the incorrect value, enter the correct value, and press Return or Enter to save it.

build the budget worksheet

- A dialog like the one shown below may appear when entering values in a worksheet. Clicking Yes in this dialog converts the worksheet into an Excel list. Click No to dismiss the dialog without making the conversion.

calculate a difference p. 33

- In Excel, all formulas begin with an equals sign (=).
- Although you can write a formula that subtracts one number from another, using cell references in the formula ensures that the formula's results remain correct, even if referenced cells' values change.
- As our formula is written, if the actual amount is lower than the budgeted amount, the difference appears as a negative number. You can make this appear as a positive number by switching the order of the cell references so the formula is =B3-C3.

calculate a percent diff p. 34

- The number of decimal places that appear in the results of the formula depends on the width of the column the formula is in.
- Don't worry that the percentages Excel calculates don't look like percentages. Later, in Chapter 6, we'll format the worksheet so the numbers look like percentages.
- If the budgeted amount in a cell is 0, the formula for the percent difference will display the error message #DIV/0! Enter this formula in cell E3 to prevent that error:
 =IF(ISERR(D3/B3),0,D3/B3)
 This rather complex formula uses logic to determine whether the formula results in an error and, if it does, results in 0.

sum some values pp. 35–36

- The SUM function is probably Excel's most used function. It can be used to add up any range of values.
- Excel is not case-sensitive when evaluating functions. You can type SUM, sum, Sum, or even sUm when you write the formula and Excel will understand.

build the budget worksheet

extra bits

- Excel 2004 for Mac OS includes a background error-checking feature that may mark cell B27 with a green error indicator. Activate the cell and click the button that appears to display a menu of error-checking options.

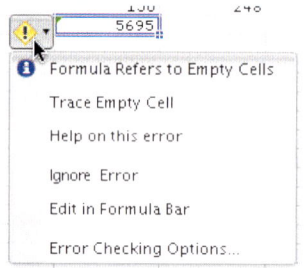

  Since this formula is not in error, choose Ignore Error to remove the error indicator.

copy and paste p. 39

- On Mac OS, you must press the Enter key (as opposed to the Return key) to paste to a selected cell. The Enter key is commonly found on the numeric keypad of a keyboard but may be located elsewhere, especially on PowerBook and iBook keyboards. Pressing Return merely moves the cell pointer down one cell.

- The Paste Options button appears when you use the Paste command. Clicking this button displays a menu of options you can use immediately after pasting one or more cells.

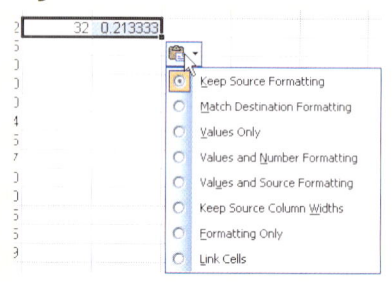

use the fill handle pp. 40–42

- The Auto Fill Options button appears when you use the fill handle to copy formulas. Clicking this button displays a menu of options you can use immediately after filling cells.

46 build the budget worksheet

change a value p. 43

- You can use this technique to change any label, value, or formula in a worksheet cell.
- To delete the contents of a cell, activate the cell, press Backspace (Windows) or Delete (Mac OS), and press Enter (Windows) or Return (Mac OS). Don't use the Spacebar to delete a cell's contents; this merely replaces its contents with a space character.

4. duplicate the worksheet

So far, we've created a budget worksheet for one month. Our project, however, includes budget worksheets for three months.

While you could simply repeat the steps in Chapter 3 twice to create two more worksheets, there is a better—and quicker—way. You can duplicate the January worksheet, clear out the values you entered, and enter new values for February. You can then do the same thing for March.

In this chapter, we'll do just that. But just to make things interesting, we'll add and remove a couple of expense categories. As you'll see, this will make the consolidation process in Chapter 5 a bit more challenging.

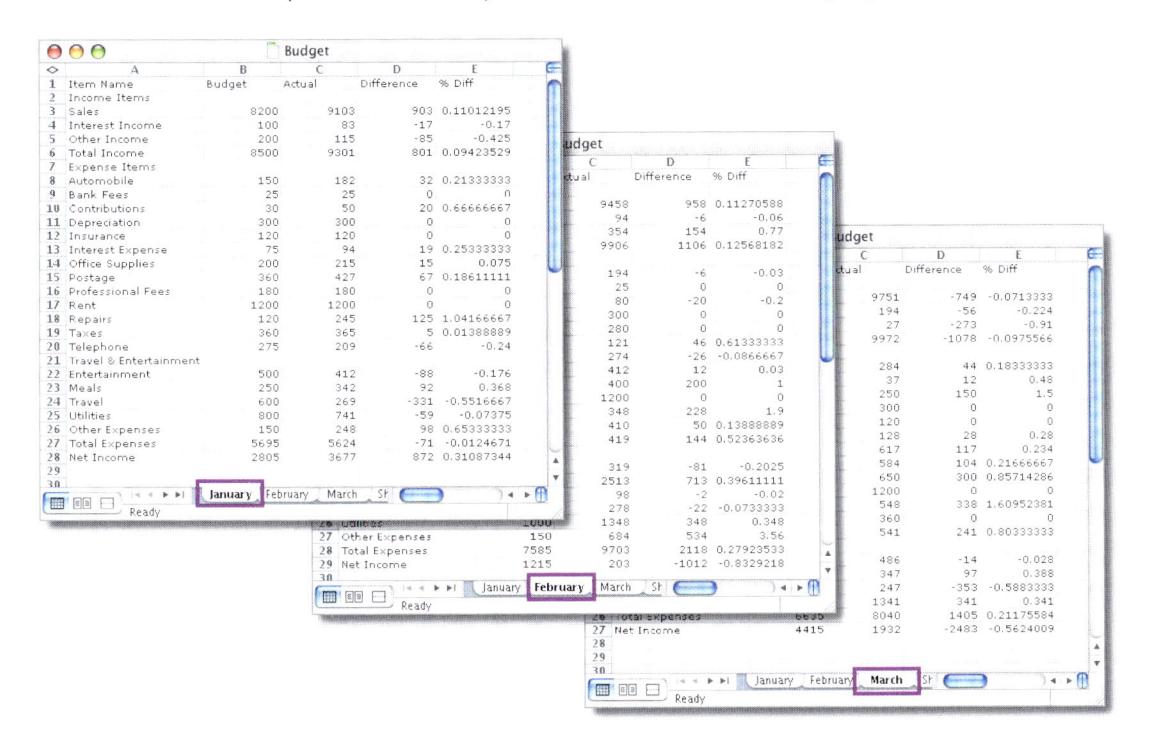

49

copy the sheet

Excel offers several ways to copy a worksheet. The quickest and easiest way is to drag the sheet tab.

1 Click the tab for the sheet you want to duplicate—in this case, the one we named January— to activate it.

2 Position the mouse pointer on the sheet tab.

3 Hold down the Ctrl (Windows) or Option (Mac OS) key and drag the sheet tab to the right.

As you drag, a tiny page icon with a plus sign in it appears at the mouse pointer and a triangle appears to indicate where the duplicate sheet will appear among the sheet tabs.

4 When the triangle appears between the sheets named January and Sheet2, release the mouse button.

A new sheet named January (2) appears.

5 Repeat steps 1–4 to duplicate the worksheet again, placing the copy between January (2) and Sheet2. The new copy is named January (3).

6 Follow the instructions on page 24 to rename January (2) to February and January (3) to March.

duplicate the worksheet

clear the values

At this point, all three sheets are identical except for their names. We need to clear out the values in the February and March sheets, leaving the labels and formulas, so we can enter new values. Because the two sheets are identical and the values are in the same cells in both sheets, we can clear the values in both sheets at the same time.

1 Click the February tab to activate that sheet.

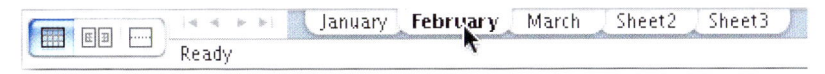

2 Hold down the Ctrl (Windows) or Command (Mac OS) key and click the March tab.

Both tabs become selected (they turn white)…

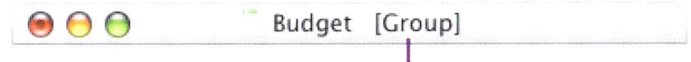

…and [Group] appears beside the workbook name in the title bar.

3 Position the mouse pointer on cell B3, press the mouse button, and drag down to cell C5 to select all of the cells with income values.

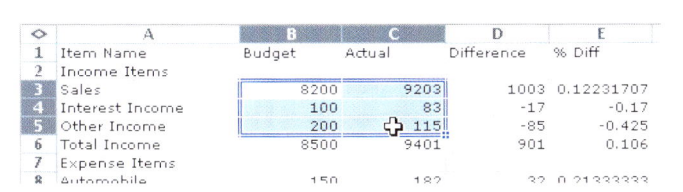

4 Choose Contents from the Clear submenu under the Edit menu.

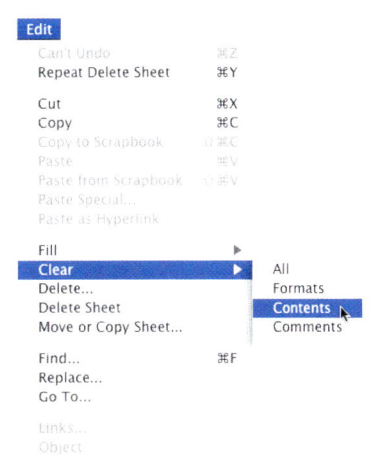

duplicate the worksheet 51

clear the values (cont'd)

The cells' contents are removed.

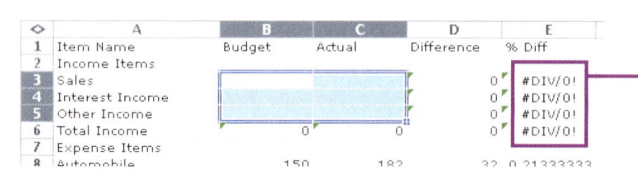

Don't worry about these errors; they'll go away when you fill in new values.

5 Position the mouse pointer on cell B8, press the mouse button, and drag down to cell C26 to select all of the cells with expense values.

6 Choose Contents from the Clear submenu under the Edit menu (shown on previous page).

The cells' contents are removed.

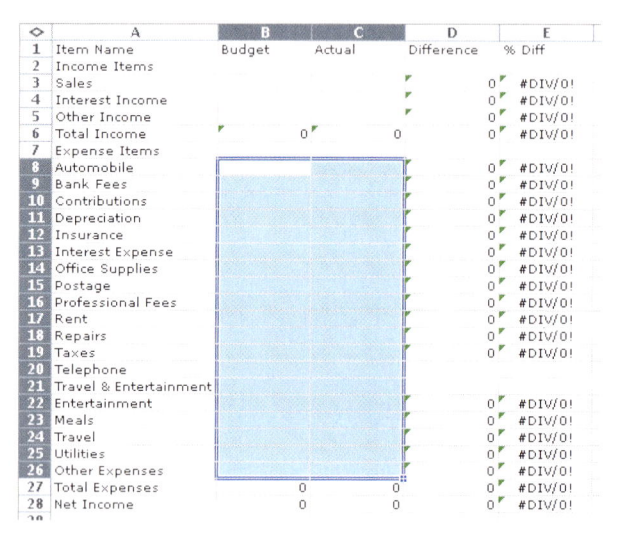

7 Click the January tab to clear the group selection. You can then click the February tab to work with just that worksheet.

52   **duplicate the worksheet**

insert a row

February is the month when the big company party is held. Although expenses for this party are part of Entertainment expenses, we want to track the party's budgeted and actual expenses on a separate line. To do this, we need to insert a new row between rows 22 and 23 (Entertainment and Meals).

1 Click the February sheet tab to activate that sheet.

2 Position the mouse pointer on the row heading for row 23. It turns into an arrow pointing to the right.

3 Click once. The entire row becomes selected.

4 Choose Rows from the Insert menu.

A new row is inserted beneath row 22 and all the rows beneath it shift down.

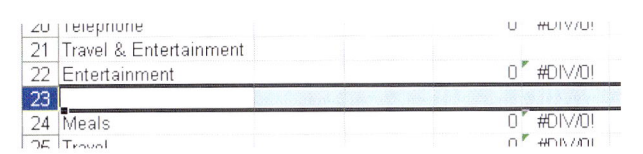

5 Make sure cell A23 is active—if it isn't, click it.

6 Type Annual Party and press Enter (Windows) or Return (Mac OS).

duplicate the worksheet   **53**

delete a row

The accountant has laid down the law. No more categorizing expenses as Other Expenses. Starting in March, he wants all expenses properly categorized in one of the other existing expense categories. That means we need to delete the row for Other Expenses.

1 Click the March sheet tab to activate that sheet.

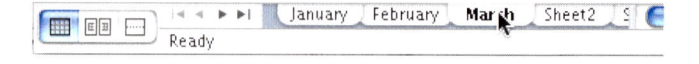

2 Position the mouse pointer on the row heading for row 26. It turns into an arrow pointing to the right.

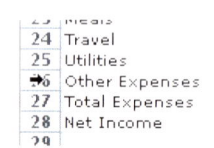

3 Click once. The entire row becomes selected.

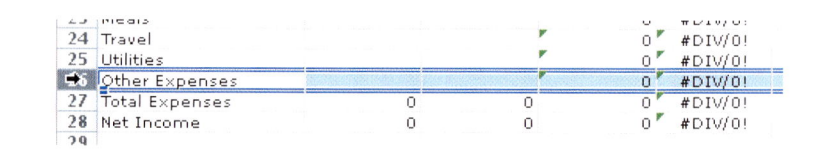

4 Choose Delete from the Edit menu.

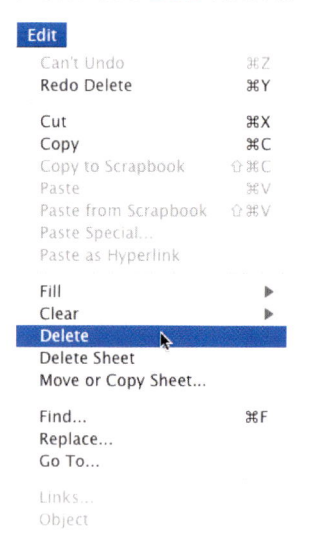

The selected row is deleted and all the rows beneath it shift up.

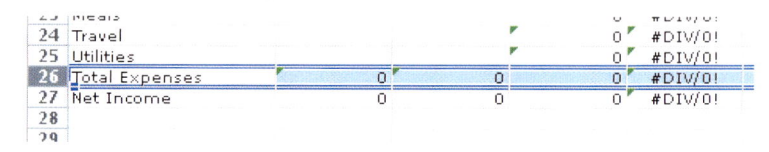

54   duplicate the worksheet

enter new values

The February and March worksheets are ready for their values. We'll follow the same basic steps on pages 31–32 to create entry areas and enter the data. To prevent ourselves from accidentally overwriting the formulas in cells B6 and C6, we'll create two separate entry areas for each worksheet.

1 Click the February sheet tab to activate that sheet.

2 Drag from cell B8 to C27 to select that range of cells.

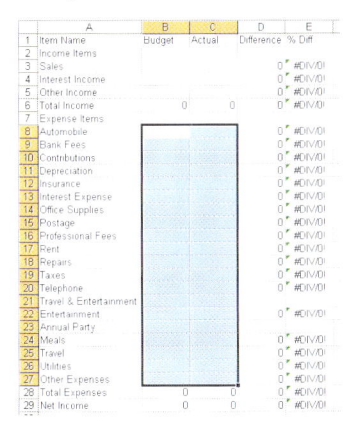

3 Hold down the Ctrl (Windows) or Command (Mac OS) key and drag from cell B3 to C5 to add that range to the selection.

Note that the active cell is the first cell in the second selection.

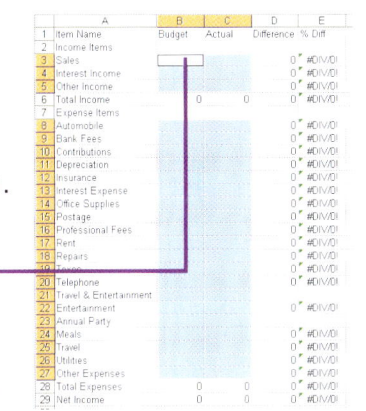

4 Enter the values shown here in each cell. Be sure to press Enter (Windows) or Return (Mac OS) to advance from one cell to the next. Pay attention; Excel will go through the cells in the top selection before it begins activating cells in the bottom selection.

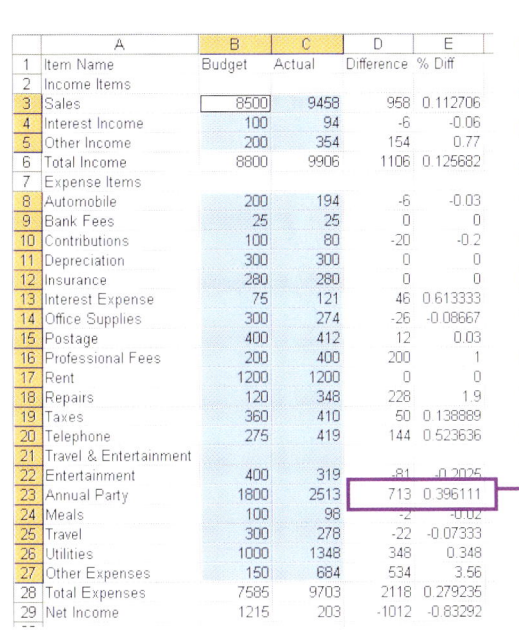

Excel automatically copies formulas to the blank row when you enter values into it.

duplicate the worksheet 55

enter new values (cont'd)

5 Click the March sheet tab to activate that sheet.

6 Repeat steps 2-4 for cells B8 to C25 and B3 to C5, entering the values shown here.

	A	B	C	D	E
1	Item Name	Budget	Actual	Difference	% Diff
2	Income Items				
3	Sales	10500	9751	-749	-0.07133
4	Interest Income	250	194	-56	-0.224
5	Other Income	300	27	-273	-0.91
6	Total Income	11050	9972	-1078	-0.09756
7	Expense Items				
8	Automobile	240	284	44	0.183333
9	Bank Fees	25	37	12	0.48
10	Contributions	100	250	150	1.5
11	Depreciation	300	300	0	0
12	Insurance	120	120	0	0
13	Interest Expense	100	128	28	0.28
14	Office Supplies	500	617	117	0.234
15	Postage	480	584	104	0.216667
16	Professional Fees	350	650	300	0.857143
17	Rent	1200	1200	0	0
18	Repairs	210	548	338	1.609524
19	Taxes	360	360	0	0
20	Telephone	300	541	241	0.803333
21	Travel & Entertainment				
22	Entertainment	500	486	-14	-0.028
23	Meals	250	347	97	0.388
24	Travel	600	247	-353	-0.58833
25	Utilities	1000	1341	341	0.341
26	Total Expenses	6635	8040	1405	0.211756
27	Net Income	4415	1932	-2483	-0.5624

Have you been saving your work?

Now is a good time to click the Save button on the Standard toolbar to save your work up to this point.

extra bits

copy the sheet p. 50
- I explain how to identify the sheet tab for an active sheet on page 24.
- If you drag a sheet tab without holding down the Ctrl (Windows) or Option (Mac OS) key, you'll change the sheet's position among the sheet tabs rather than copy it.

clear the values pp. 51–52
- In Excel 2004 for Mac OS, when you clear out the values, you may see green markers in the corners of cells that reference those values. That's Excel's automatic error-checking feature. Ignore them; they will disappear when you enter new values.
- Don't believe that you cleared out the contents of two worksheets at once? Click the sheet tabs for February and March to see for yourself!
- It's important to remove the group sheet selection as instructed in step 6 before entering new values in the February worksheet. Otherwise, you'll enter the same values in both the February and March worksheets.

insert a row p. 53
- The Rows command under the Insert menu inserts as many rows as you have selected above the selected row(s). So if you select three rows and use this command, it will insert three rows above the first selected row.
- If you select a column by clicking on its column heading, you can use the Columns command on the Insert menu to insert a column to the left of it.
- Excel automatically rewrites formulas as necessary when you insert a row or column.

delete a row p. 54
- If you select a column by clicking on its column heading, you can use the Delete command on the Edit menu to delete it.
- Excel automatically rewrites formulas as necessary when you delete a row or column.

duplicate the worksheet 57

5. consolidate the results

We now have three worksheets full of budget and actual information. Our next step is to consolidate this information into one summary worksheet for the quarter. We'll do that with Excel's consolidation feature.

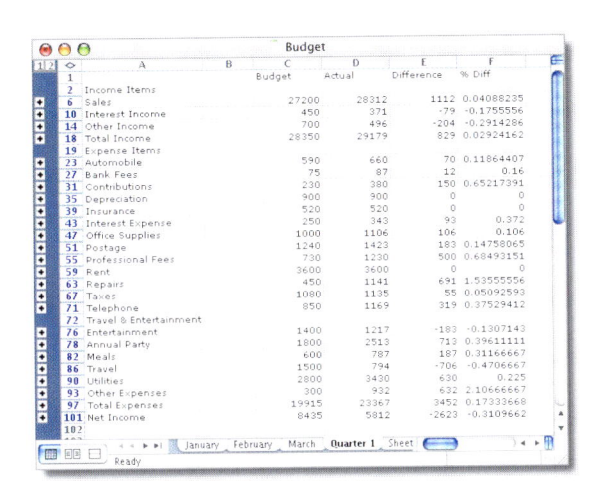

prepare the sheet

The consolidated information will go on its own sheet. We can prepare the sheet by activating it, renaming it, and activating the first cell of the consolidation range.

1 Click the sheet tab for Sheet2 to activate it.

2 Follow the instructions on page 24 to name the sheet tab Quarter 1.

3 Activate cell A1.

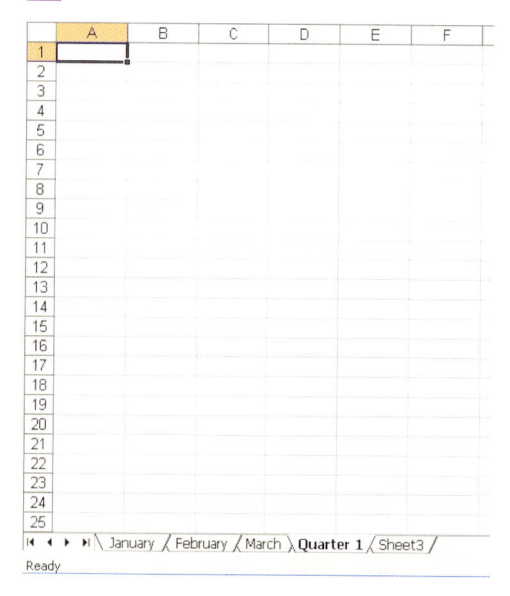

consolidate the results

consolidate

Excel's consolidation feature uses the Consolidate dialog to collect your consolidation settings, including the worksheet ranges you want to include in the consolidation and the type of consolidation you want to perform.

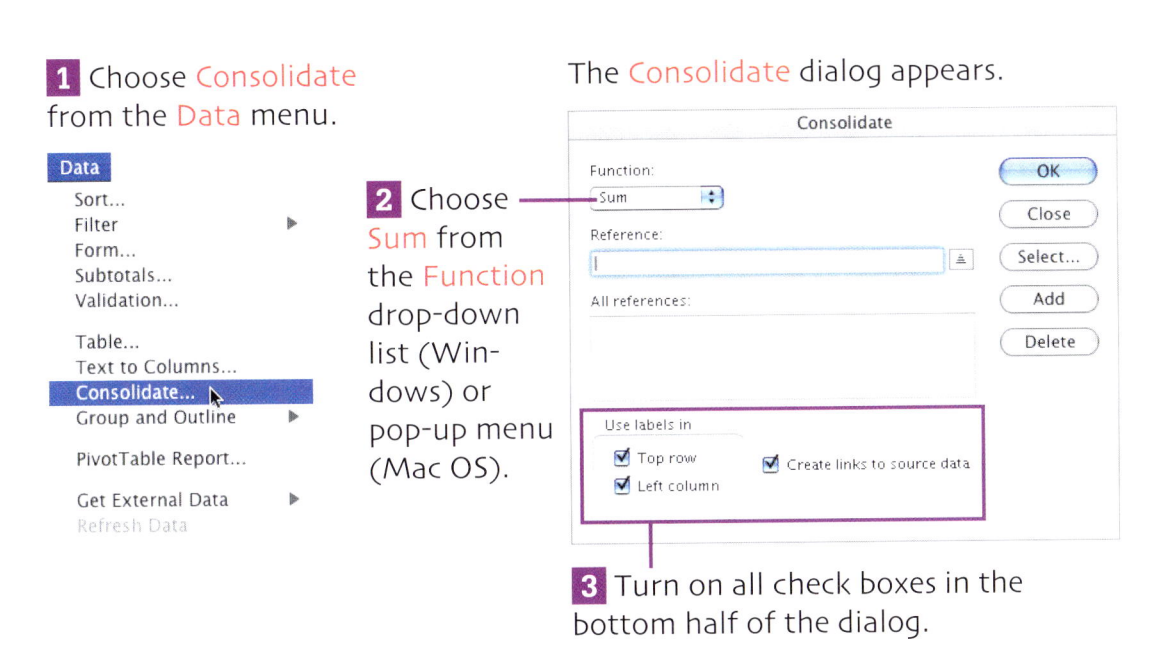

1 Choose Consolidate from the Data menu.

2 Choose Sum from the Function drop-down list (Windows) or pop-up menu (Mac OS).

The Consolidate dialog appears.

3 Turn on all check boxes in the bottom half of the dialog.

4 Click the January sheet tab so that sheet becomes active behind the dialog. January! appears in the Reference box.

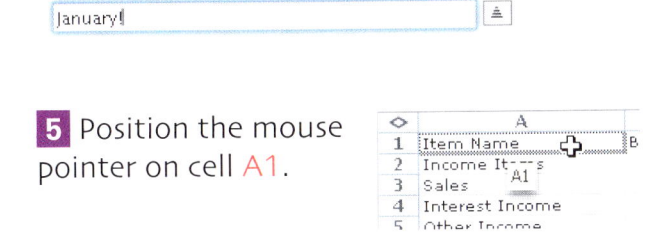

5 Position the mouse pointer on cell A1.

consolidate the results **61**

consolidate (cont'd)

6 Press the mouse button and drag down and to the right to select from cell A1 to cell D28. As you drag, the Consolidate dialog collapses so you can see what you're doing and a selection marquee appears around the cells you drag over.

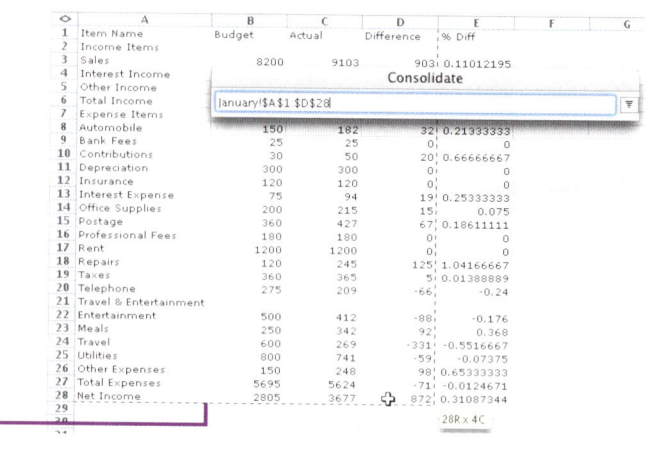

selection marquee

7 Release the mouse button. The range you selected appears in the Reference box.

8 Click Add. The reference is copied to the All references box.

9 Click the February sheet tab to activate that sheet. February!$A$1:$D$28 appears in the Reference box and a selection marquee in the worksheet behind the dialog indicates that range of cells.

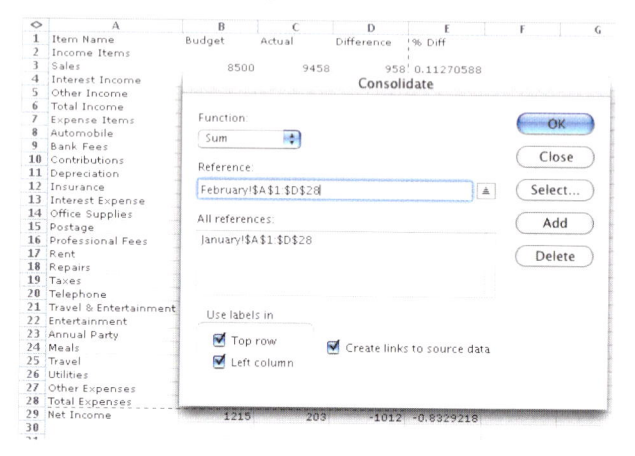

10 Position the mouse pointer on cell A1.

consolidate the results

11 Press the mouse button and drag down and to the right to select from cell A1 to cell D29. As you drag, the Consolidate dialog collapses.

12 Release the mouse button. The range you selected appears in the Reference box.

13 Click Add. The reference is copied to the All references box.

14 Click the March sheet tab so that sheet becomes active. March!$A$1:$D$29 appears in the Reference box and a selection marquee in the worksheet indicates that range of cells.

15 Position the mouse pointer on cell A1.

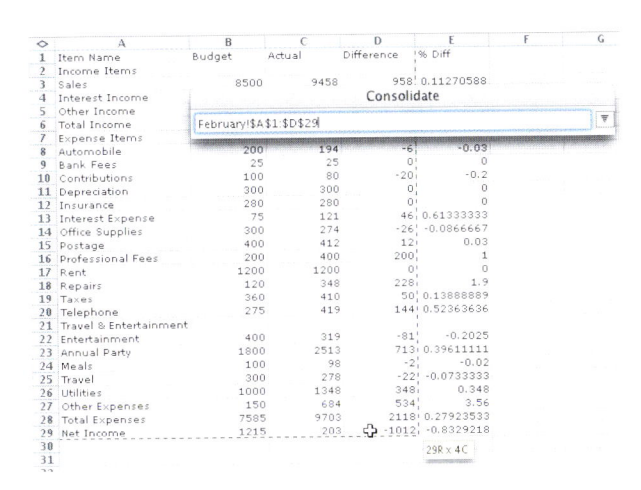

16 Press the mouse button and drag down and to the right to select from cell A1 to cell D27. As you drag, the Consolidate dialog collapses.

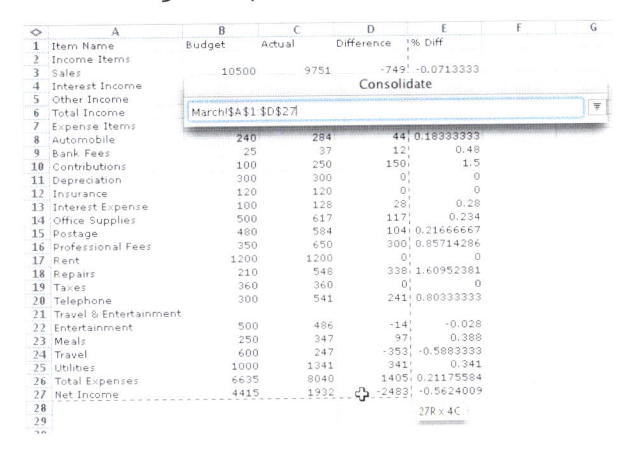

consolidate the results

63

consolidate (cont'd)

17 Release the mouse button. The range you selected appears in the Reference box.

18 Click Add. The reference moves to the All references box.

19 Click OK.

At this point, the Consolidate dialog should look like this.

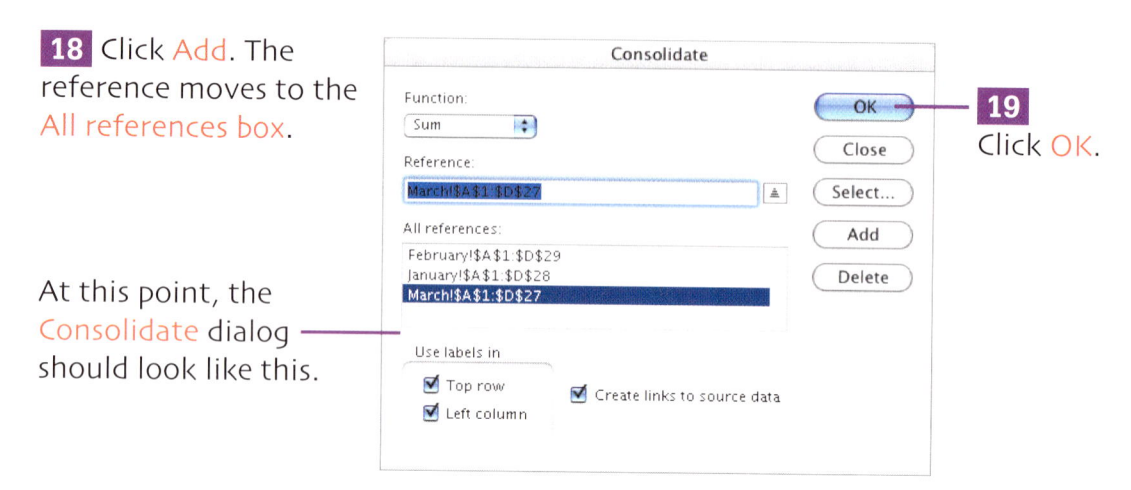

Excel creates the consolidation and displays it in the Quarter 1 worksheet.

outline symbols

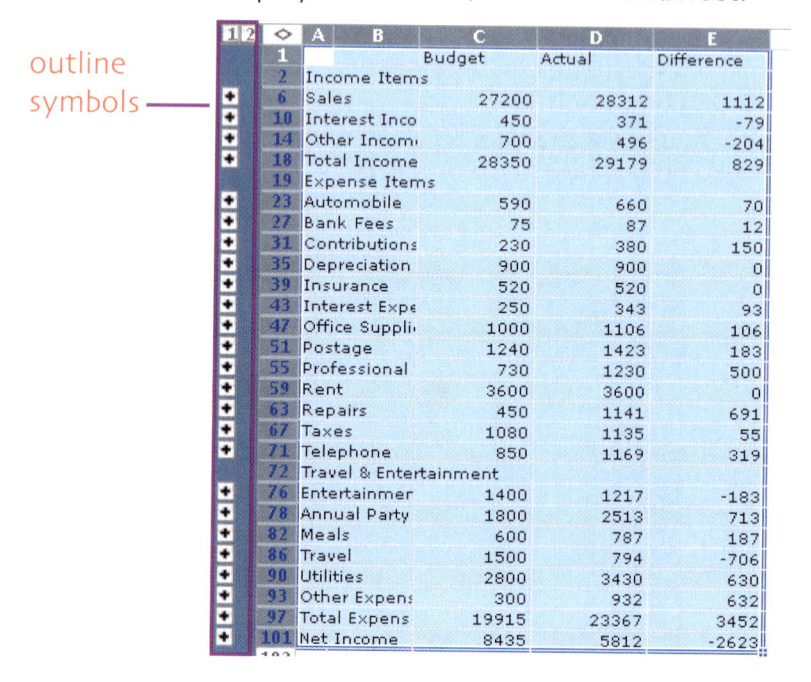

64 consolidate the results

check the consolidation

When you consolidate multiple worksheets as instructed here, you create a new worksheet with "3-D" references to the source worksheets. Because Excel has to display contents from all of the source cells, it automatically displays the consolidation as an outline with the outline collapsed so only the total for each category appears.

Double-click the right border of column A's heading to widen the column.

Click an outline symbol to display or hide rows.

Excel enters the name of the source workbook in column B. In this example, all source data is in Budget.

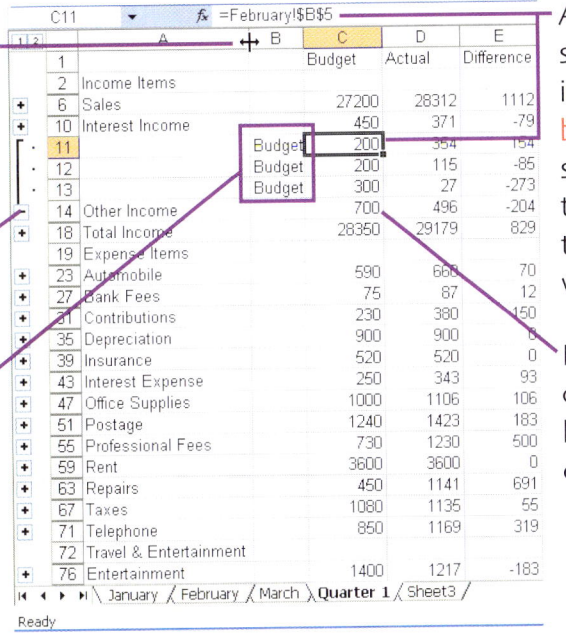

Activate a cell to see its formula in the formula bar. This example shows a reference to a cell in the February worksheet.

Excel places the category total beneath the detail.

If one of the source worksheets changes, the consolidation automatically changes.

consolidate the results 65

calculate percent diff

When we created our consolidation, we omitted the percent difference calculation on the source worksheets. The reason: Our consolidation used the SUM function to add values in the source worksheets. Adding the percentages would result in incorrect values for the consolidated percent differences. As a result, we need to recreate the percent difference formula in the consolidation worksheet and copy it to the appropriate cells.

1 Click the sheet tab for the Quarter 1 worksheet to activate that sheet.

2 Enter % Diff in cell F1 and press Enter (Windows) or Return (Mac OS).

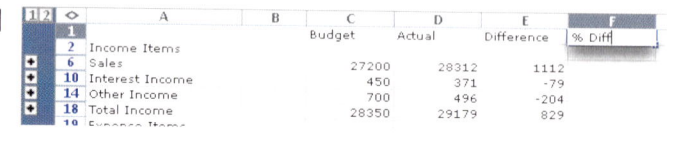

3 Enter the formula =E6/C6 in cell F6. You can either type it in or follow the procedure on page 34 to enter the formula by typing and clicking. (If you do click, be sure to click in the correct cells!) Don't forget to press Enter or Return to complete the formula.

4 Use techniques on pages 39–42 to copy the formula to cells F10 to F18, F23 to F71, and F76 to F101.

When you're finished, it should look like this.

Save your work.

Click the Save button on the Standard toolbar.

66   consolidate the results

extra bits

consolidate pp.61–64

- Because each worksheet in the consolidation has a slightly different organization—remember, we added a row in one and deleted a row in another—you must turn on the Left column check box to properly consolidate. Doing so tells Excel to sum values based on category name (the row label) rather than row position.

calculate percent diff p.66

- If you use the fill handle to copy the formula in cell F6 to other cells, Excel automatically copies the formula to cells in hidden rows you drag over. This doesn't really matter, though, since we're only interested in the consolidated numbers and will keep the hidden rows hidden.

6. format worksheets

Although the information in our four worksheets is accurate and informative, it doesn't look very good. And in this day and age, looks are almost everything. We need to dress these worksheets up to make them more presentable.

Excel offers many extremely flexible formatting options. Our worksheets can benefit from some font and number formatting, as well as alignment, borders, and color. As shown here, we'll transform our plain Jane worksheets into worksheets that demand attention.

On the following pages, I'll show you how to apply formatting to the January worksheet. You can repeat those steps on your own for the other worksheets in our workbook.

Before

	A	B	C	D	E
1	Item Name	Budget	Actual	Difference	% Diff
2	Income Items				
3	Sales	8200	9103	903	0.11012195
4	Interest Income	100	83	-17	-0.17
5	Other Income	200	115	-85	-0.425
6	Total Income	8500	9301	801	0.09423529
7	Expense Items				
8	Automobile	150	182	32	0.21333333
9	Bank Fees	25	25	0	0
10	Contributions	30	50	20	0.66666667
11	Depreciation	300	300	0	0
12	Insurance	120	120	0	0
13	Interest Expense	75	94	19	0.25333333
14	Office Supplies	200	215	15	0.075
15	Postage	360	427	67	0.18611111
16	Professional Fees	180	180	0	0
17	Rent	1200	1200	0	0
18	Repairs	120	245	125	1.04166667
19	Taxes	360	365	5	0.01388889
20	Telephone	275	209	-66	-0.24
21	Travel & Entertainment				
22	Entertainment	500	412	-88	-0.176
23	Meals	250	342	92	0.368
24	Travel	600	269	-331	-0.5516667
25	Utilities	800	741	-59	-0.07375
26	Other Expenses	150	248	98	0.65333333
27	Total Expenses	5695	5624	-71	-0.0124671
28	Net Income	2805	3677	872	0.31087344

After

	A	B	C	D	E
1	Item Name	Budget	Actual	Difference	% Diff
2	Income Items				
3	Sales	$8,200.00	$9,103.00	$903.00	11.0%
4	Interest Income	100.00	83.00	-17.00	-17.0%
5	Other Income	200.00	115.00	-85.00	-42.5%
6	Total Income	$8,500.00	$9,301.00	$801.00	9.4%
7	Expense Items				
8	Automobile	$150.00	$182.00	$32.00	21.3%
9	Bank Fees	25.00	25.00	0.00	0.0%
10	Contributions	30.00	50.00	20.00	66.7%
11	Depreciation	300.00	300.00	0.00	0.0%
12	Insurance	120.00	120.00	0.00	0.0%
13	Interest Expense	75.00	94.00	19.00	25.3%
14	Office Supplies	200.00	215.00	15.00	7.5%
15	Postage	360.00	427.00	67.00	18.6%
16	Professional Fees	180.00	180.00	0.00	0.0%
17	Rent	1,200.00	1,200.00	0.00	0.0%
18	Repairs	120.00	245.00	125.00	104.2%
19	Taxes	360.00	365.00	5.00	1.4%
20	Telephone	275.00	209.00	-66.00	-24.0%
21	Travel & Entertainment				
22	Entertainment	500.00	412.00	-88.00	-17.6%
23	Meals	250.00	342.00	92.00	36.8%
24	Travel	600.00	269.00	-331.00	-55.2%
25	Utilities	800.00	741.00	-59.00	-7.4%
26	Other Expenses	150.00	248.00	98.00	65.3%
27	Total Expenses	$5,695.00	$5,624.00	-$71.00	-1.2%
28	Net Income	$2,805.00	$3,677.00	$872.00	31.1%

set font formatting

Font formatting changes the way individual characters of text appear. By default, Excel 2003 for Windows uses 10 point Arial font; Excel 2004 for Mac OS uses 10 point Verdana font. You can change the font settings applied to any combination of worksheet cells.

In our worksheets, we'll make the column and row headings bold and larger so they really stand out. We'll also change the font applied to the entire worksheet to something a little more interesting.

1 Drag to select cells A1 to A28.

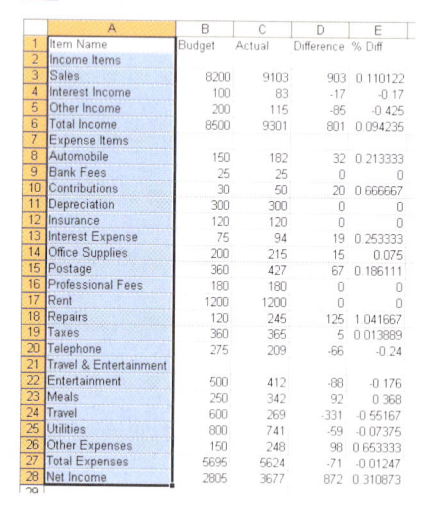

2 Hold down the Ctrl (Windows) or Command (Mac OS) key and drag to add cells B1 to E1 to the selection.

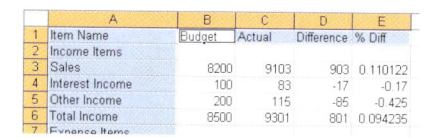

3 Click the Bold button on the Formatting toolbar (Windows) or the Formatting Palette (Mac OS).

The text in the selected cells turns bold.

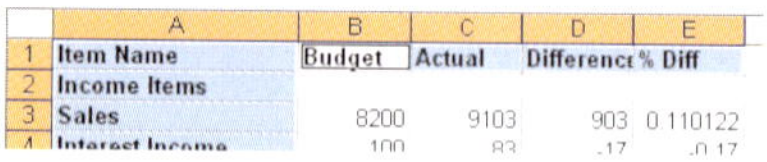

4 Choose 11 from the Font Size drop-down list on the Formatting toolbar (Windows) or Formatting Palette (Mac OS).

format worksheets

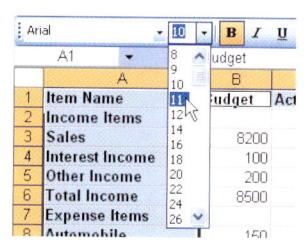

The text in the selected cells gets larger.

5 Click the Select All button in the top corner of the worksheet grid to select all cells in the worksheet.

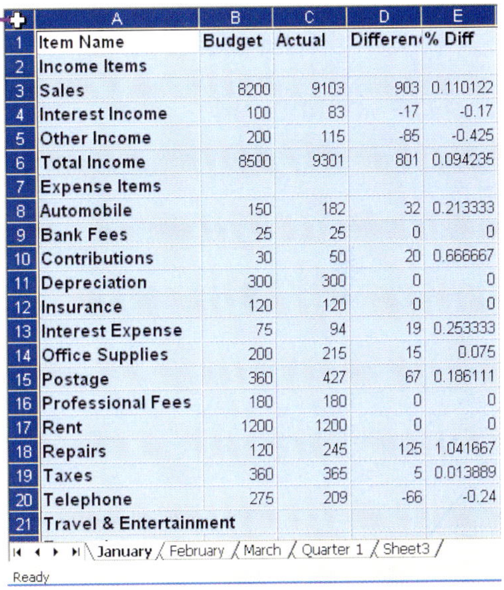

6 Choose Lucida Sans from the Font drop-down list on the Formatting toolbar (Windows) or Formatting Palette (Mac OS).

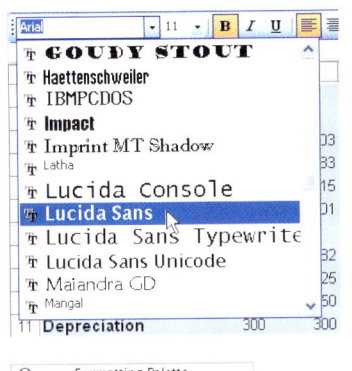

The text in the selected cells changes to the Lucida Sans font.

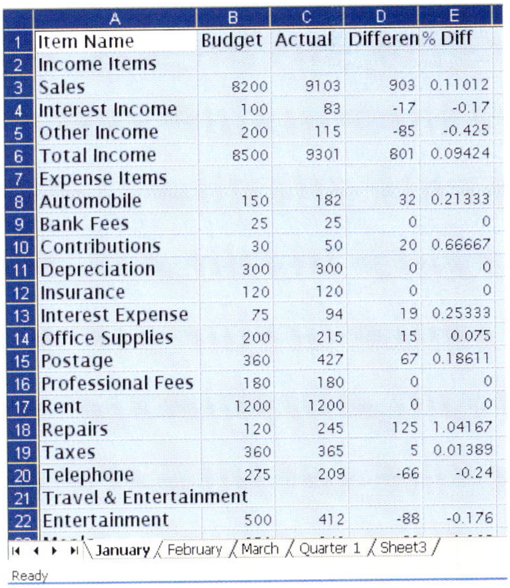

format worksheets

71

format values

The dollar amounts in our worksheets would be a lot easier to read with commas and dollar signs.

1 Drag to select all cells containing numbers in columns B, C, and D.

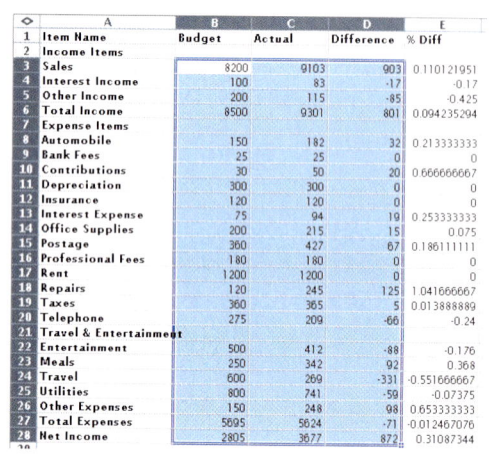

2 In Windows, click the Comma Style button on the Formatting toolbar. Then skip ahead to the top of the next page.

2 In Mac OS, choose Cells from the Format menu.

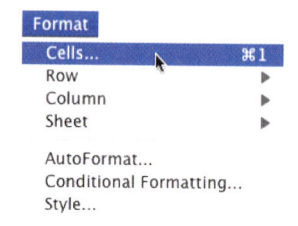

The Format Cells dialog appears.

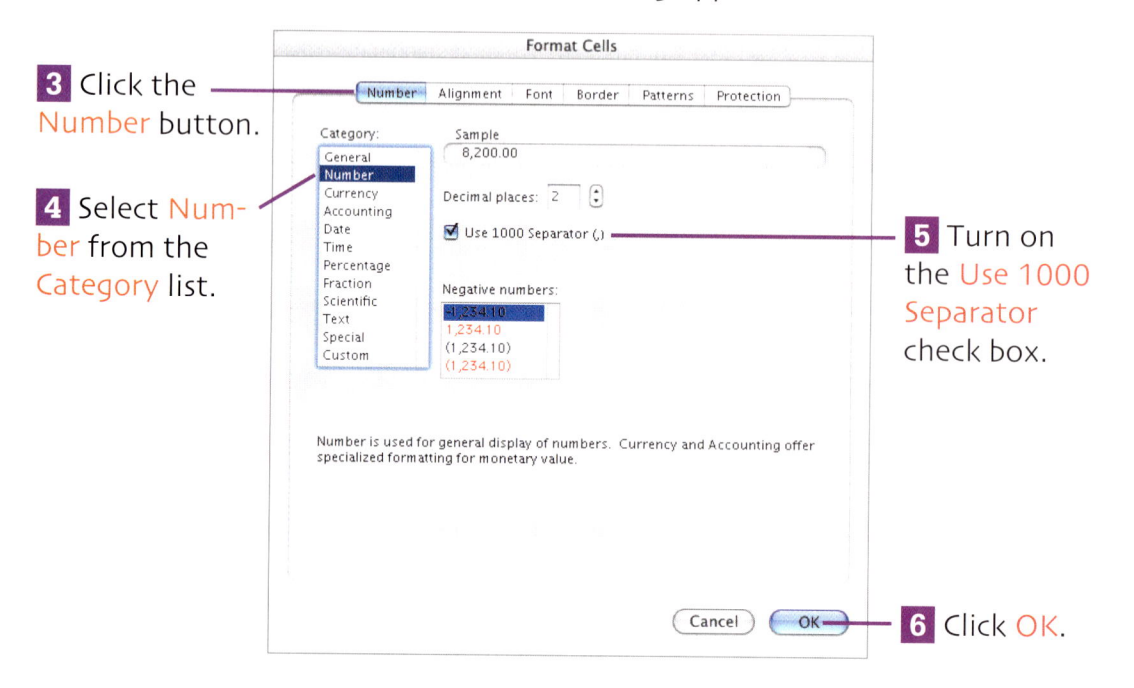

3 Click the Number button.

4 Select Number from the Category list.

5 Turn on the Use 1000 Separator check box.

6 Click OK.

72

format worksheets

Commas and decimal places appear as appropriate for all values in selected cells.

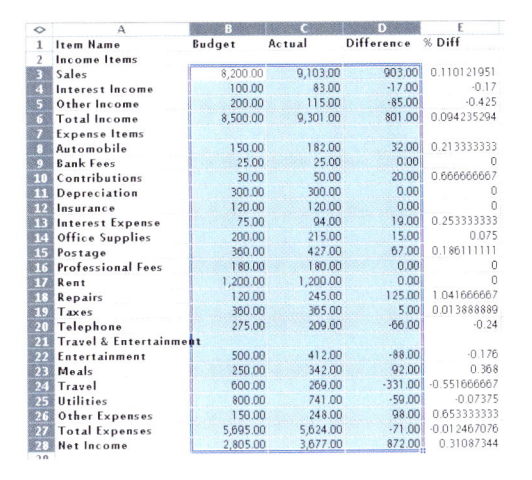

8 Click the Currency Style button in the Formatting toolbar (Windows) or choose Currency from the Format drop-down list in the Formatting Palette (Mac OS).

Currency symbols appear beside values in the selected cells.

7 Drag to select cells B3 to D3, B6 to D6, B8 to D8, and B27 to D28. Remember you must hold down the Ctrl (Windows) or Command (Mac OS) key to select multiple ranges.

format worksheets 73

format percentages

We can also use number formatting to format the percentages in column E so they look like percentages.

1 Drag to select all cells containing numbers in column E.

2 Click the Percent Style button on the Formatting toolbar (Windows) or choose Percentage from the Format drop-down list on the Formatting Palette (Mac OS).

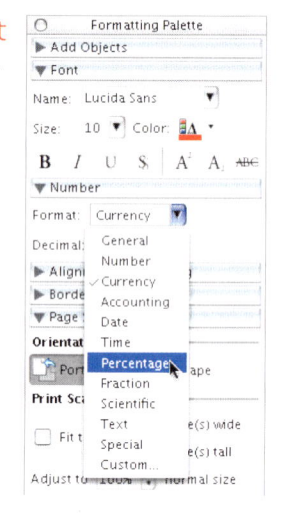

In Windows, the numbers are formatted as percentages without any decimal places.

In Mac OS, the numbers are formatted as percentages with two decimal places.

(I think Microsoft makes these minor differences between the Windows and Mac OS versions of the software just to drive software book authors crazy.)

74 format worksheets

3 Click the Increase Decimal button on the Formatting toolbar (Windows) or the Decrease Decimal button on the Formatting Palette (Mac OS).

The numbers are reformatted so there's one decimal place.

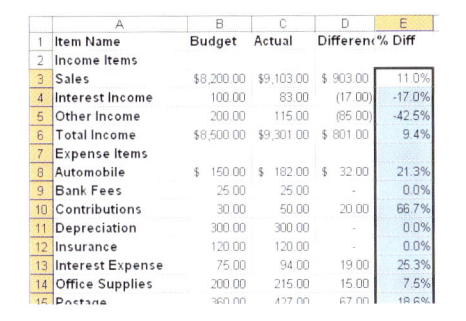

format worksheets 75

set column widths

When you create a worksheet, Excel automatically sets a default width for columns. The width of columns in the Windows version of Excel is 8.43 characters (or 64 pixels). The width of columns in the Mac OS version of Excel is 10 characters (or 1.04 inches).

We've already used the AutoFit feature to increase the width of column A so its text fits in the column. And, if you use the Windows version of Excel, you may have noticed that it widened one or two columns to accommodate the number formatting we applied.

Now we'll make column A a little wider again—remember, we increased the text size and applied bold formatting, which make the text take up more space. We'll also set the width of columns B, C, D, and E to a consistent wider setting.

1 Double-click the right border of column A.

The column automatically widens again to accommodate the widest text in the column.

2 Position the mouse pointer on the column heading for column B. It turns into an arrow pointing down.

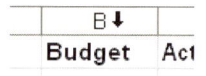

76   format worksheets

3 Press the mouse button and drag to the right to select columns B, C, D, and E.

4 Choose Width from the Column submenu under the Format menu.

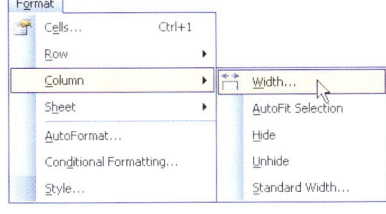

The Column Width dialog appears.

5 In Windows, enter 12 in the text box and click OK...

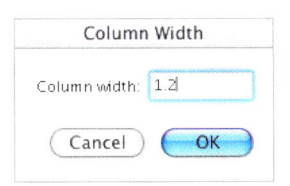

...or in Mac OS, enter 1.2 in the text box and click OK.

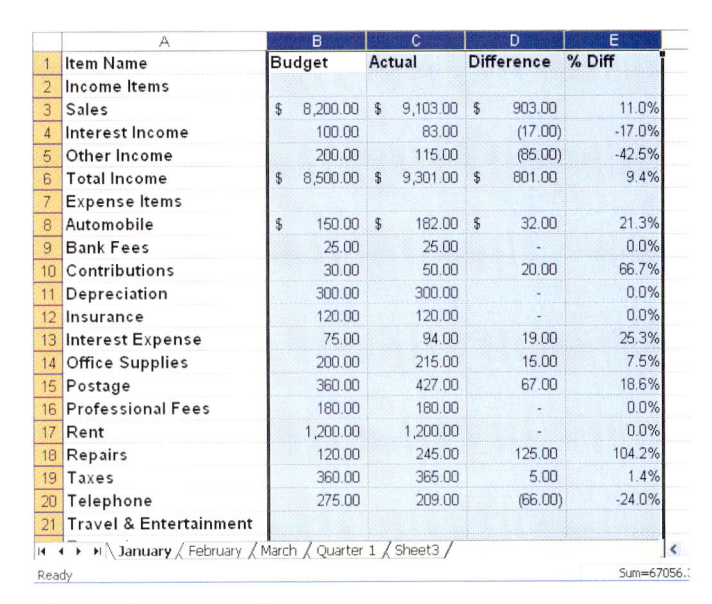

The columns widen.

format worksheets   **77**

set alignment

By default, text is left-aligned in a cell and a number (including a date or time) is right-aligned in a cell. For our worksheet, the headings at the top of columns B, C, D, and E might look better if they were centered.

1 Drag to select cells B1 through E1.

2 Click the Center button on the Formatting toolbar (Windows)…

…or the Align Center button in the Alignment and Spacing area of the Formatting Palette (Mac OS).

You may have to click here to display Alignment and Spacing options.

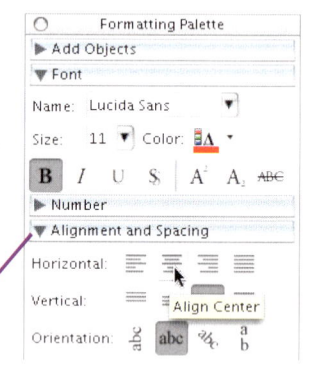

The cell contents are centered between the cell's left and right boundaries.

78   format worksheets

indent text

Entertainment, Meals, and Travel are three row headings that are part of the major Travel & Entertainment category of expenses. We can make that clear to the people who view the worksheet by indenting those three row headings.

1 Select cells A22 through A24.

2 Click the Increase Indent button on the Formatting toolbar (Windows)…

…or enter 1 in the Indent box in the Alignment and Spacing area of the Formatting Palette and press Return (Mac OS).

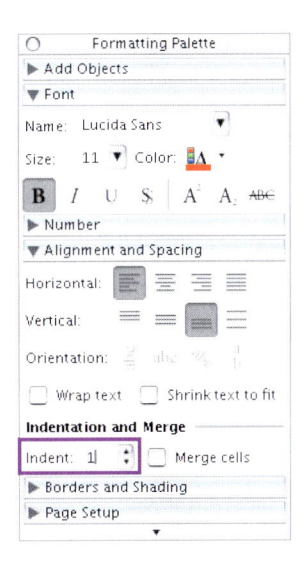

Each cell's contents are shifted to the right.

Save your work.

Click the Save button on the Standard toolbar.

format worksheets 79

add borders

Borders above and below the totals and net amounts would really help them stand out. We'll add single lines above and below Income and Expense totals and a double line beneath the Net Income amounts.

1 Select cells B6 to E6, and B27 to E27. Remember, you must hold down the Control (Windows) or Command (Mac OS) key to select multiple ranges.

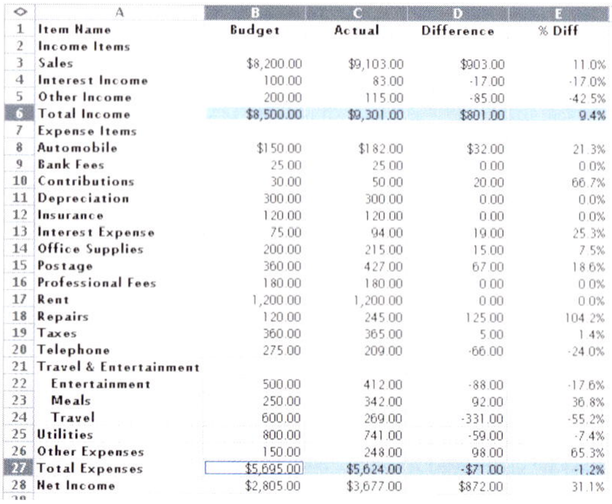

In Windows:

2 Click the triangle on the Borders button on the Formatting toolbar to display a menu of options.

3 Choose the Top and Bottom Border button.

In Mac OS:

2 Click the triangle on the Type button in the Borders and Shading area of the Formatting Palette to display a menu of options.

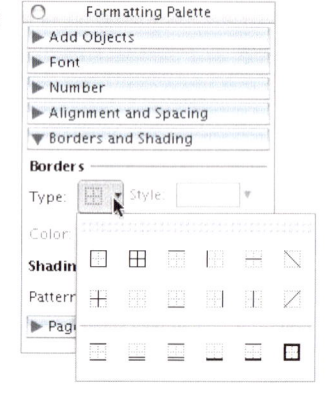

3 Choose the Top and Bottom Border button.

80   format worksheets

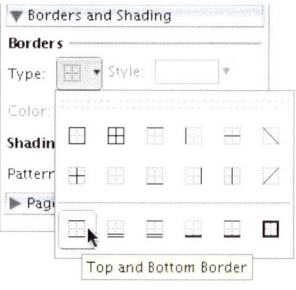

Borders are applied to the top and bottom of all selected cells.

4 Select cells B28 to E28.

In Windows:

5 Click the triangle on the Borders button on the Formatting toolbar to display a menu of options.

6 Choose the Top and Double Bottom Border button.

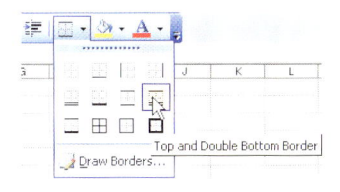

In Mac OS:

5 Click the triangle on the Type button in the Borders and Shading area of the Formatting Palette to display a menu of options.

6 Choose the Top and Double Bottom Border button.

A double border appears beneath the selected cells.

Here's what it should look like when you're done, with the selection area removed.

format worksheets 81

apply shading

Shading can also improve the appearance of a worksheet. We'll apply dark colored shading to worksheet cells containing headings so they really stand out, then apply a lighter color shading to the rest of the worksheet.

1 Select cells A1 to E1 and A2 to A28. Remember, you must hold down the Control (Windows) or Command (Mac OS) key to select multiple ranges.

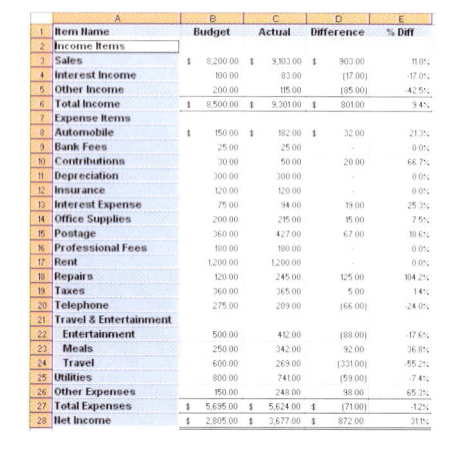

2 In Windows, click the triangle on the Fill button on the Formatting toolbar to display a menu of colors and choose a dark color…

…or in Mac OS, click the triangle on the Color button in the bottom part of the Borders and Shading area of the Formatting Palette to display a menu of colors and choose a dark color.

82 format worksheets

The color is applied to selected cells. Here's what it might look like with the selection area removed.

3 Select cells B2 to E28.

4 Follow step 2 to select a lighter color.

The color is applied to selected cells.

Save your work.

Click the Save button on the Standard toolbar.

format worksheets

83

change text color

When we applied a dark border to the worksheet's headings, we created a problem: The black text may not be legible with the dark cell shading. We can fix this problem by making the heading text a lighter color.

1 Select cells A1 to E1 and A2 to A28. Remember, you must hold down the Control (Windows) or Command (Mac OS) key to select multiple ranges.

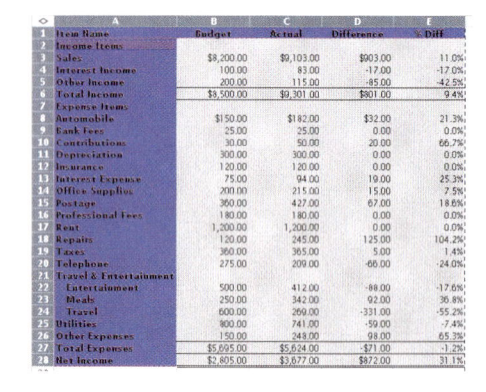

2 In Windows, click the triangle on the Font Color button on the Formatting toolbar to display a menu of colors and choose a light color…

…or in Mac OS, click the triangle on the Color button in the Font area of the Formatting Palette to display a menu of colors and choose a light color.

The color you selected is applied to the contents of selected cells. Here's what it might look like with the selection area removed.

84 format worksheets

format all worksheets

So far, all we've done is format one of the four worksheets in our workbook file: January. You can follow the steps on pages 70–84 to apply the same formatting to the other worksheets in the file: February, March, and Quarter 1.

Here are a few things to keep in mind:

- To activate a worksheet, click its sheet tab.

- Not all worksheets have the same number of columns and rows, so you won't be able to use the cell selections exactly as written in this chapter. Be sure to select the correct areas when applying formatting.

- In the February worksheet, Annual Party should be indented with the other Travel & Entertainment row headings.

- For the Quarter 1 worksheet, keep the consolidation's detail hidden. You can also hide column B by setting its column width to 0 (zero).

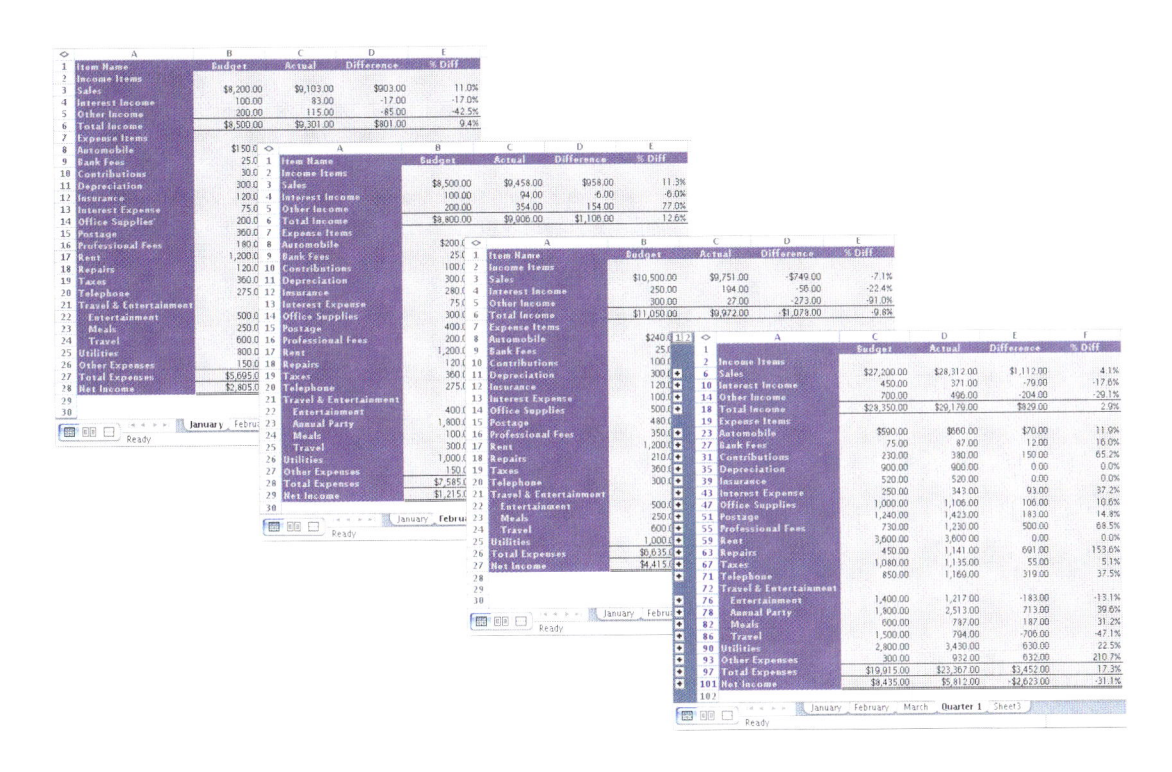

format worksheets

extra bits

set font formatting pp. 70–71

- A font is basically a typeface.
- A point is a unit of measurement roughly equal to 1/72 of an inch. Fonts are measured in points. The bigger the point size, the bigger the characters.
- Choose your font carefully! Some fonts are designed for display purposes only and can be difficult to read.
- Don't get carried away with font formatting. Too much formatting can distract the reader.
- Want more font formatting options? Choose Cells from the Format menu to display the Format Cells dialog, then click the Font tab. Use this dialog to set font formatting options and click OK to apply them to selected cells.

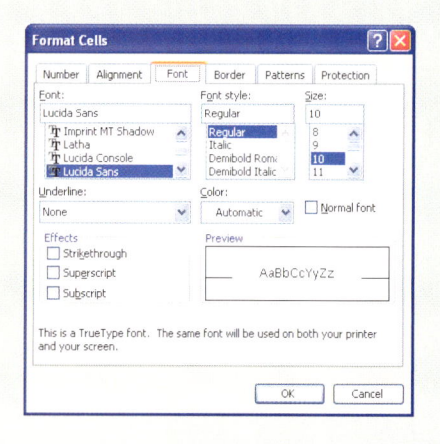

format values pp. 72–73

- Note that the number formatting applied with the Comma Style button in Windows is slightly different from the one applied with the Format Cells dialog in Mac OS as instructed on page 72.
- There are some subtle differences between number formatting as applied here in Windows and Mac OS. For example, in Windows, comma and currency formatting display dashes for zero values and put parentheses around negative values.

set column widths pp. 76–77

- In Windows, you enter column widths in characters; in Mac OS, you enter column width in inches. I don't know why they're different, but there it is.
- You can hide a column by setting its width to 0. To unhide a column, select the columns on either side of it and set the column width to anything but 0. The column reappears between the other two columns.

format worksheets

set alignment p. 78

- Depending on column width settings, you may find that column headings look better when right-aligned over the numbers beneath them rather than centered. Click the Align Right button to try it and decide for yourself.

add borders p. 80

- Don't confuse borders with underlines. Underlines are part of a cell's font formatting and, when applied, appear only beneath characters in a cell. Borders appear for the entire width of the cell.

- Don't confuse cell gridlines with borders, either. Gray cell gridlines appear onscreen to help you see cell boundaries. Normally, they don't print—although you can elect to print them in the Page Setup dialog. Cell borders always print.

7. add a chart

Excel includes a powerful and flexible charting feature that enables you to create charts based on worksheet information. Its Chart Wizard makes it easy to create charts to your specifications. Best of all, if any of the data in a source worksheet changes, the chart automatically changes accordingly.

In Excel, charts can be inserted into a workbook file in two ways:

- A chart sheet, as discussed in Chapter 2 and shown below, displays a chart on a separate workbook sheet.

- An embedded chart is a chart that is added as a graphic object to a worksheet.

In this chapter, we'll create a pie chart of actual expenses for the quarter as a separate sheet within our Budget workbook file.

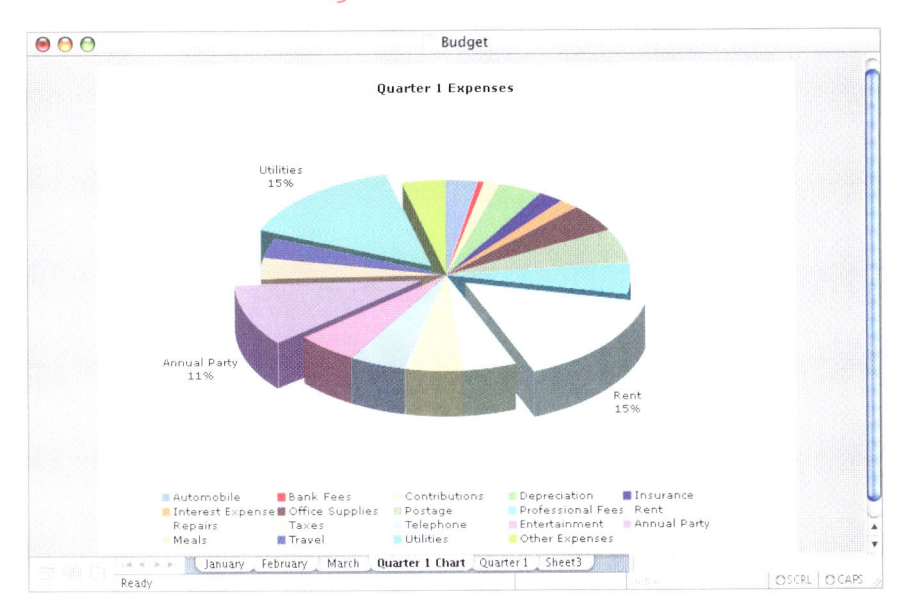

89

hide a row

Our chart will include all expense categories from the Quarter 1 file. Before we select the information to chart, however, we'll hide the row labeled Travel & Entertainment, which has no values, so it does not appear in the chart.

1 Click the Quarter 1 sheet tab to activate that sheet.

2 Click on the row heading number for row 72 to select it.

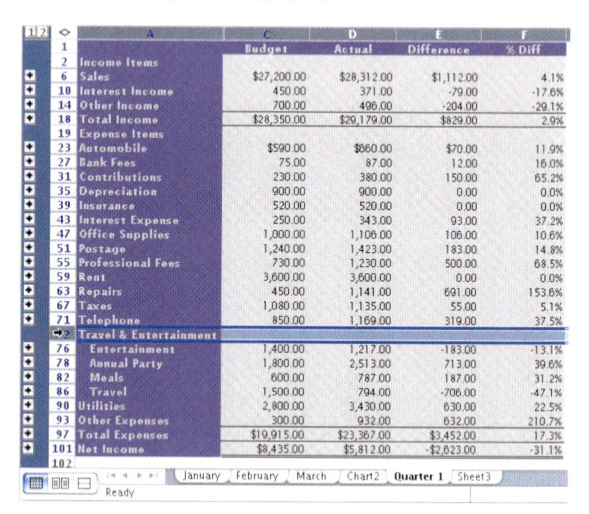

3 Choose Hide from the Row submenu under the Format menu.

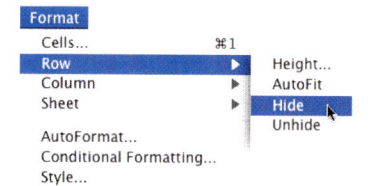

The row disappears.

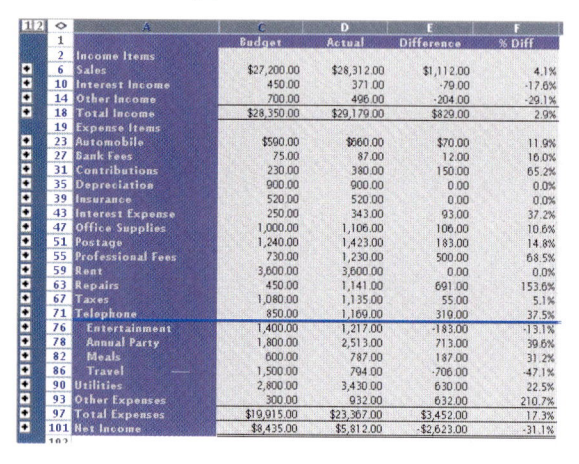

add a chart

start the chart wizard

The first step in creating a chart is to select the information you want to include in the chart. This includes both values and corresponding labels. Then start the Chart Wizard.

1 Select cells A23 to A93 and cells D23 to D93. Remember, you must hold down the Control (Windows) or Command (Mac OS) key to select multiple ranges.

2 Click the Chart Wizard button on the Standard toolbar.

Windows

Mac OS

The first step of the Chart Wizard dialog appears, as shown on the next page.

add a chart   91

select a chart type

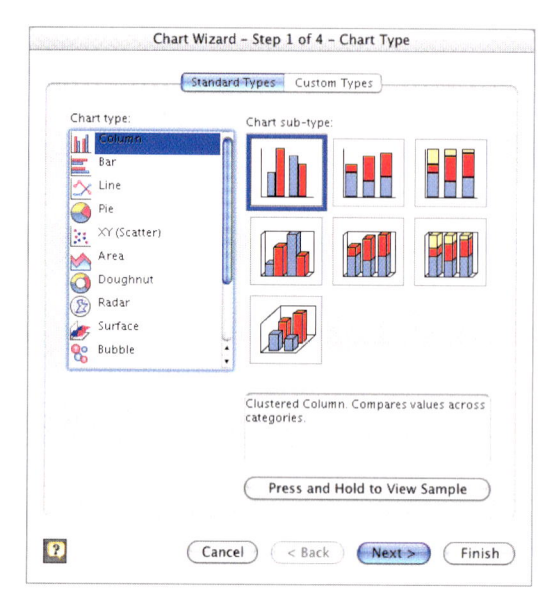

Step 1 of the Chart Wizard prompts you to select a type of chart. We'll be creating a 3-D pie chart.

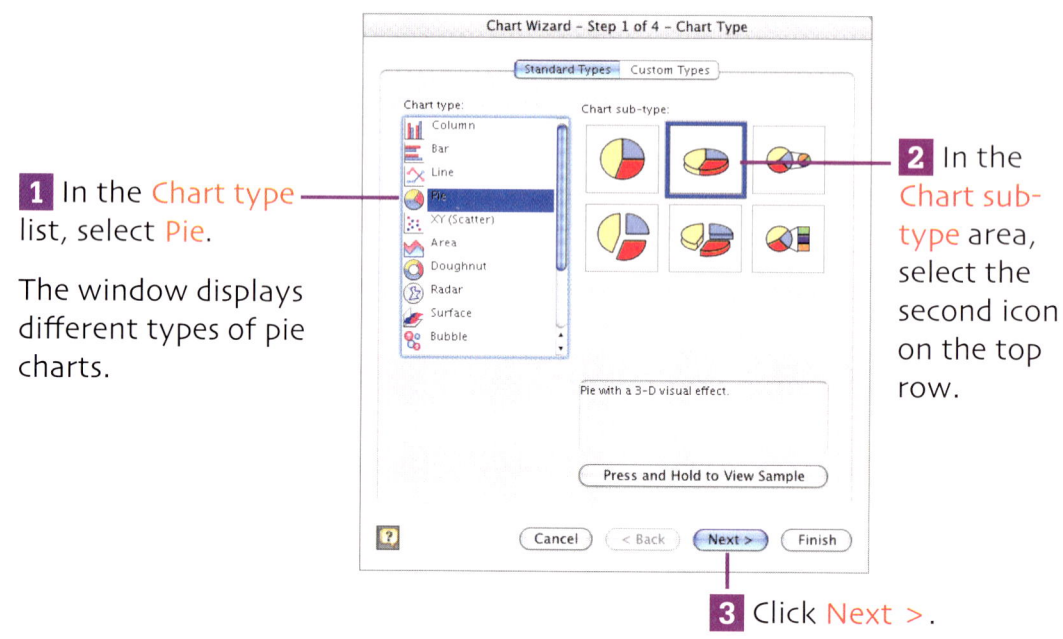

1 In the Chart type list, select Pie.

The window displays different types of pie charts.

2 In the Chart sub-type area, select the second icon on the top row.

3 Click Next >.

The second step of the Chart Wizard dialog appears, as shown on the next page.

add a chart

check the source data

Step 2 of the Chart Wizard enables you to enter the range of data to be charted. But if you correctly selected the right ranges of cells as instructed on page 91, the data range should already be entered.

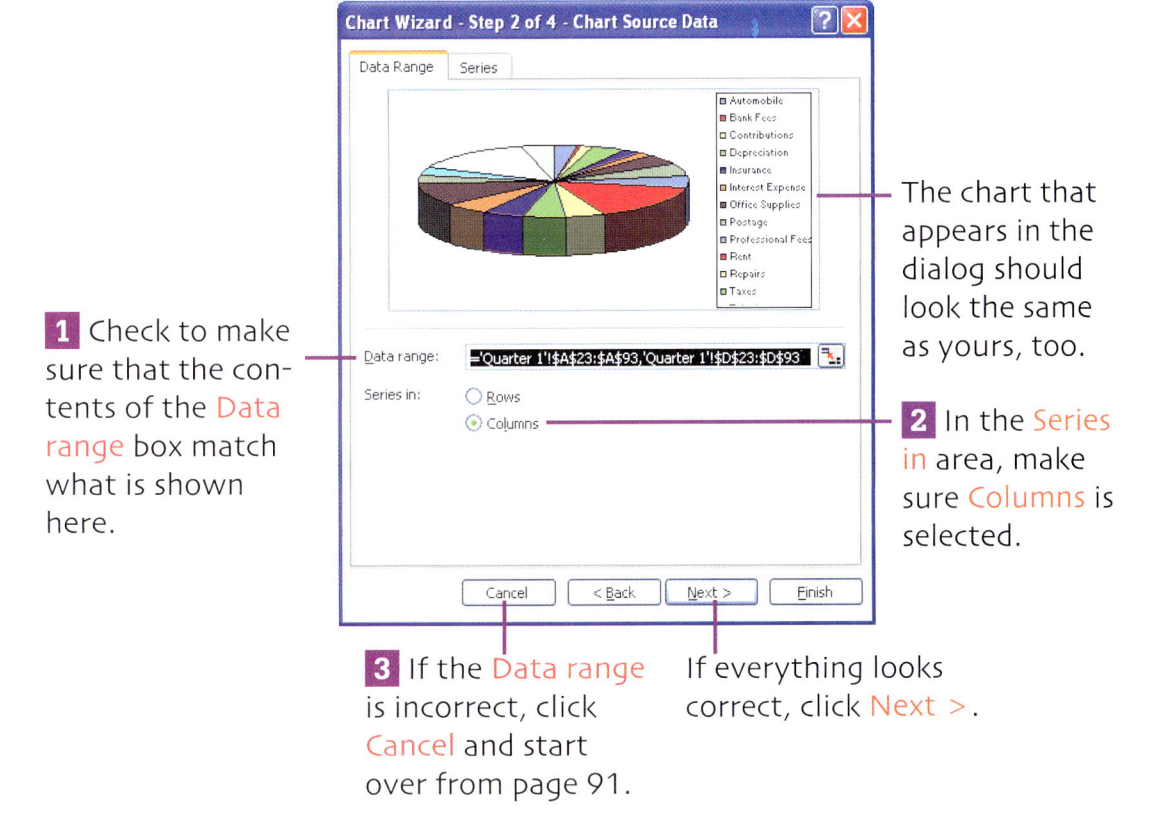

1 Check to make sure that the contents of the Data range box match what is shown here.

The chart that appears in the dialog should look the same as yours, too.

2 In the Series in area, make sure Columns is selected.

3 If the Data range is incorrect, click Cancel and start over from page 91.

If everything looks correct, click Next >.

The third step of the Chart Wizard dialog appears, as shown on the next page.

add a chart 93

set chart options

Step 3 of the Chart Wizard has three parts for setting chart options. Click a tab (Windows) or button (Mac OS) at the top of the dialog to set each type of option.

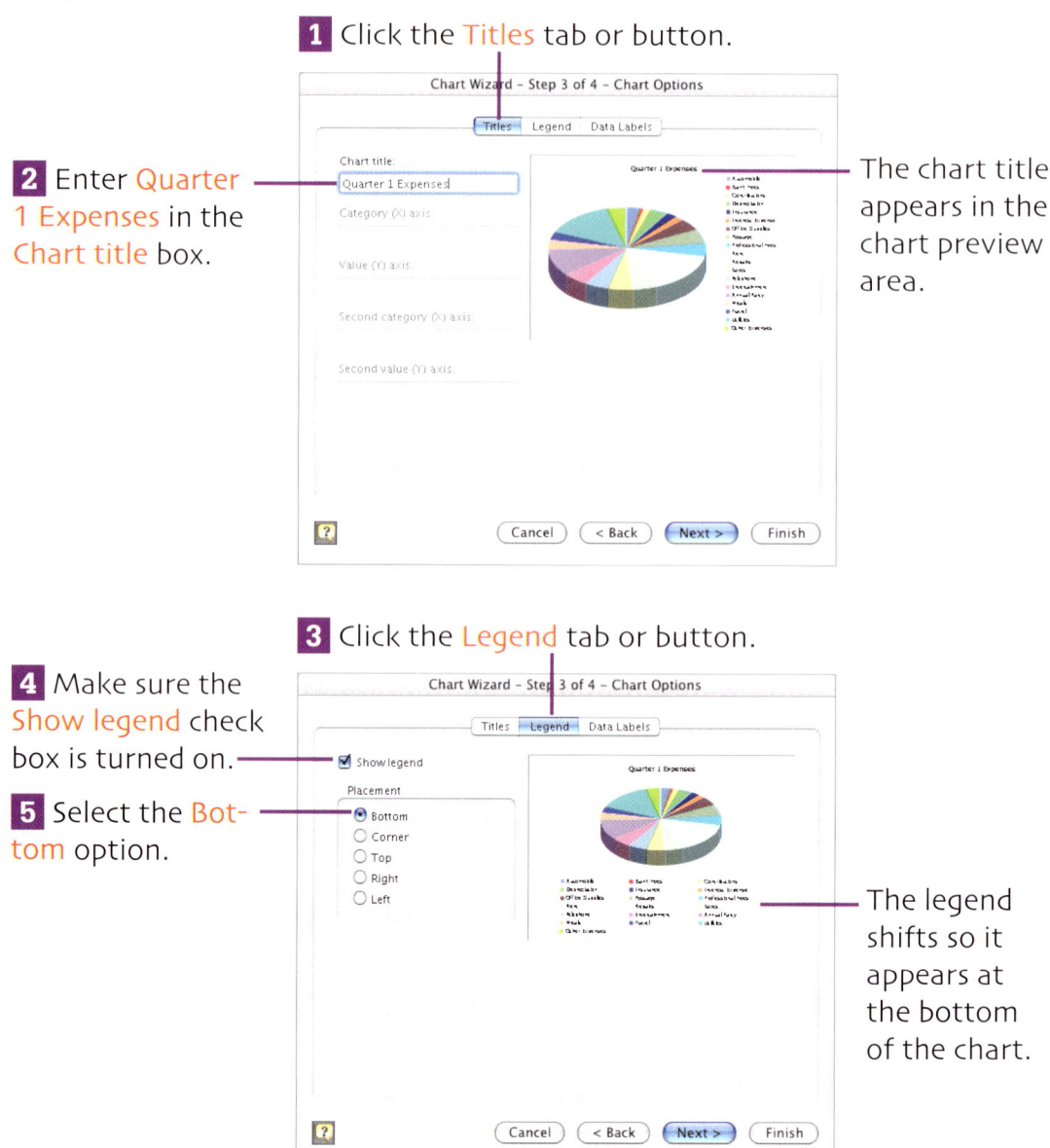

1 Click the Titles tab or button.

2 Enter Quarter 1 Expenses in the Chart title box.

The chart title appears in the chart preview area.

3 Click the Legend tab or button.

4 Make sure the Show legend check box is turned on.

5 Select the Bottom option.

The legend shifts so it appears at the bottom of the chart.

94 add a chart

6 Click the Data Labels tab or button.

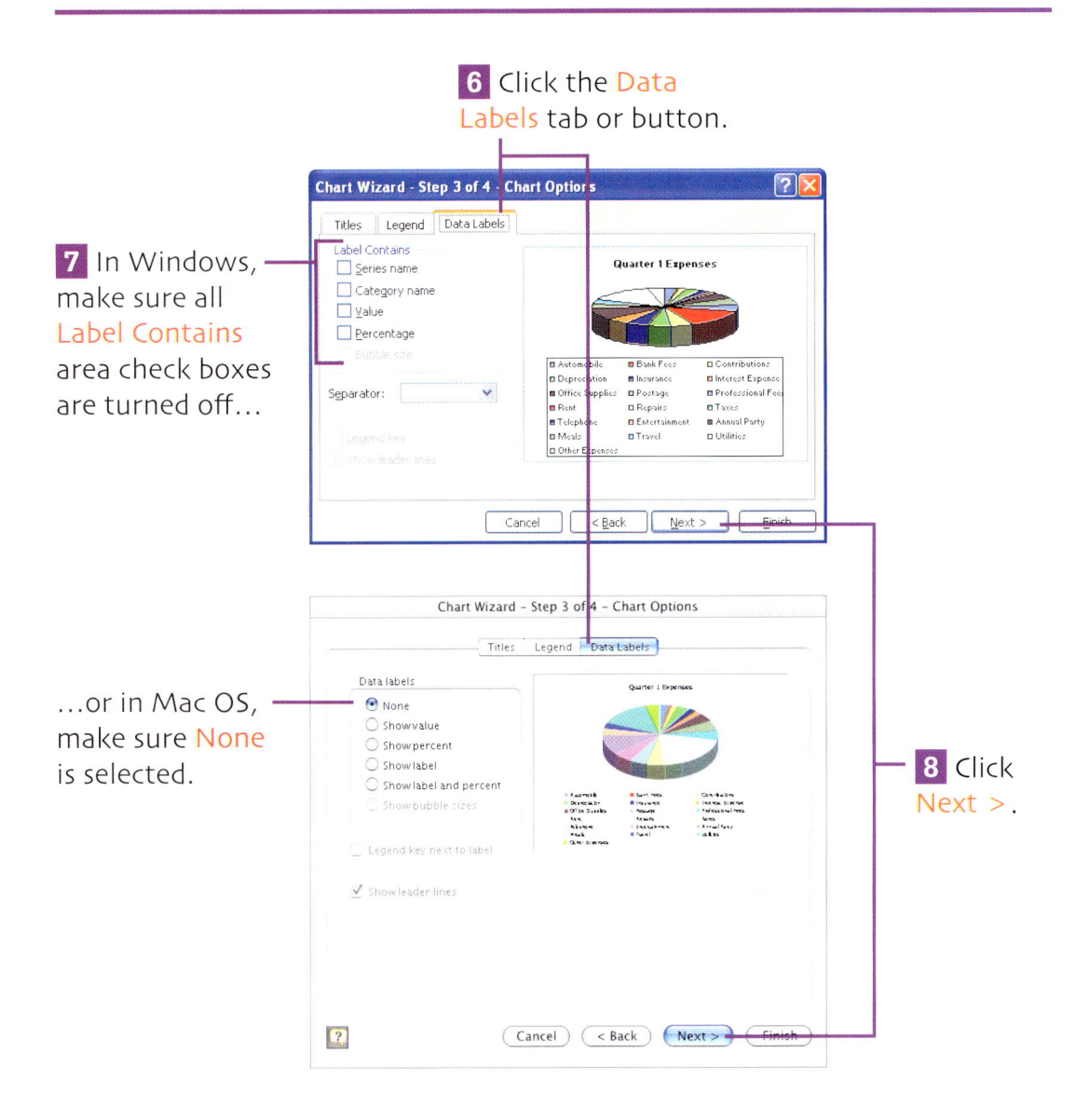

7 In Windows, make sure all Label Contains area check boxes are turned off...

...or in Mac OS, make sure None is selected.

8 Click Next >.

The fourth step of the Chart Wizard dialog appears, as shown on the next page.

add a chart

95

set the chart location

Step 4 of the Chart Wizard lets you specify whether the chart will be on its own chart sheet or inserted as an object in a worksheet. Our chart will be on its own worksheet.

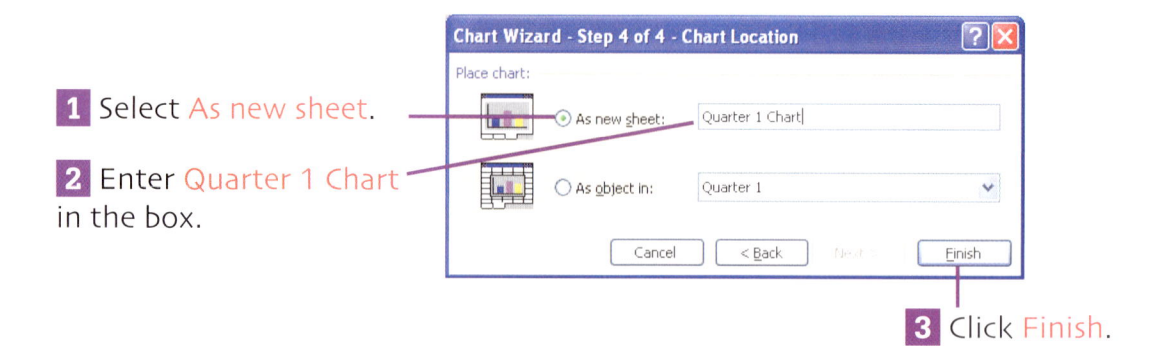

1 Select As new sheet.

2 Enter Quarter 1 Chart in the box.

3 Click Finish.

The chart appears in a chart sheet window.

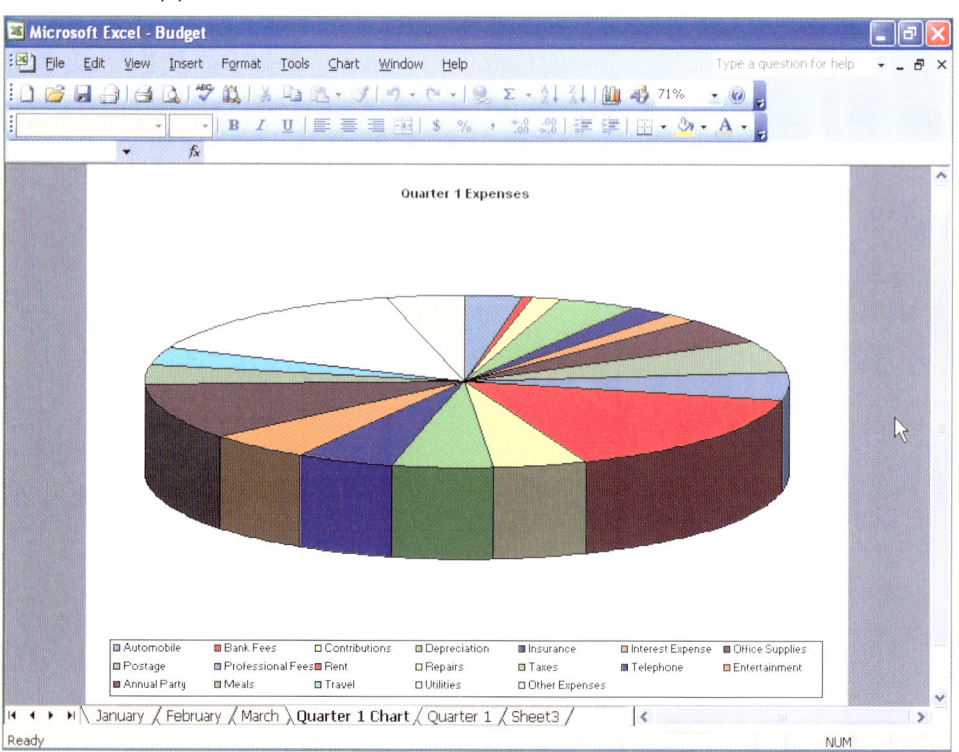

add a chart

explode a pie

You can make one or more pieces of a pie chart really stand out by "exploding" them away from the pie. In our example, we'll emphasize the pie pieces that represent the top three expense items: Rent, Utilities, and Annual Party.

1 Click the piece of pie representing Rent. (You'll know you have the right one when "Rent" appears in its tooltip.) The entire pie chart becomes selected.

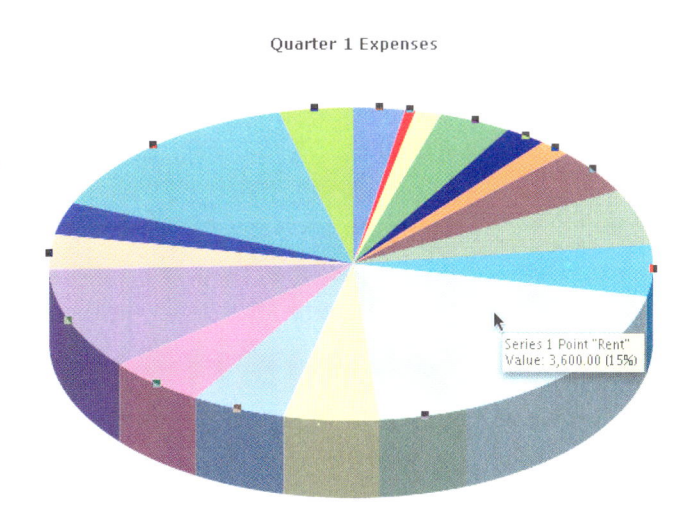

2 Click the pie piece so selection handles appear around it.

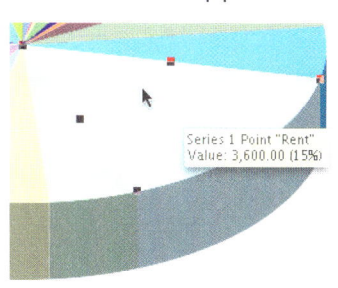

3 Drag the piece of pie away from the center of the pie. An outline of the pie moves as you drag.

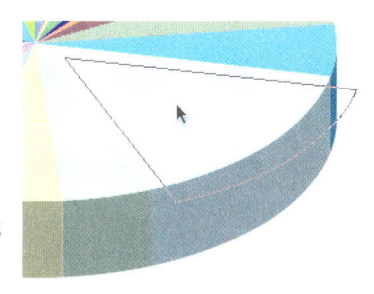

add a chart   97

explode a pie (cont'd)

4 Release the mouse button. The pie is redrawn with the piece you dragged "exploded" away.

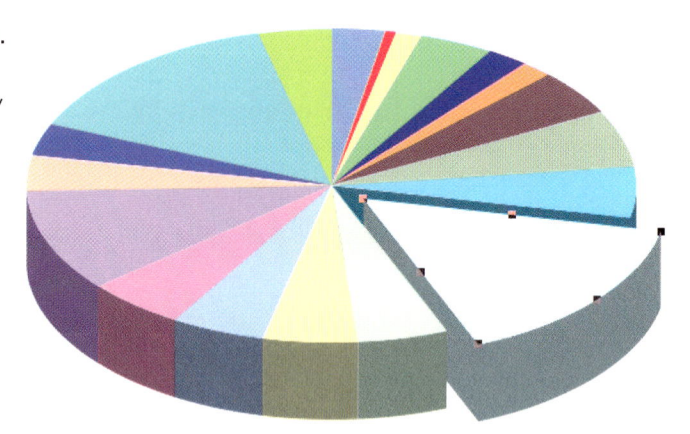

5 Repeat steps 2 through 4 for the pie pieces representing Utilities and Annual Party.

When you're finished, the pie chart should look like this.

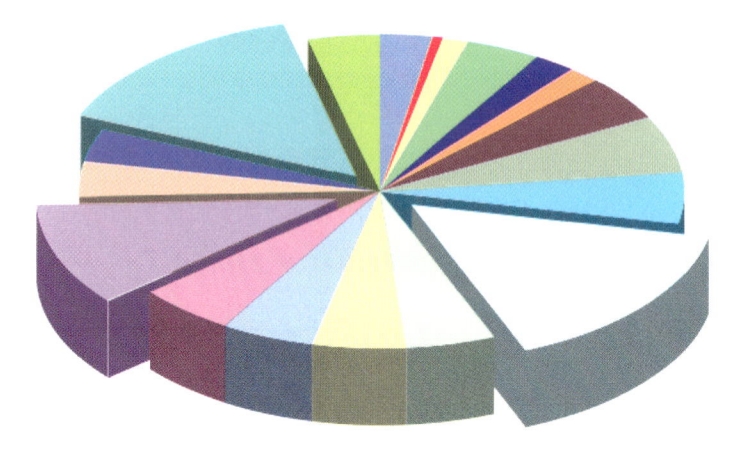

98

add a chart

add data labels

Data labels provide information about data in a chart. Although this chart includes a color-coded legend, we'll provide additional information about the three biggest expenses using data labels.

1 Click the pie piece for Rent. If the entire chart becomes selected, click it again so only the Rent piece is selected.

2 Double-click the selected pie piece.

The Format Data Point dialog appears.

Important Note: If the Format Data Series dialog appears instead, click Cancel and start over with step 1.

3 Click the Data Labels tab (Windows) or Labels button (Mac OS).

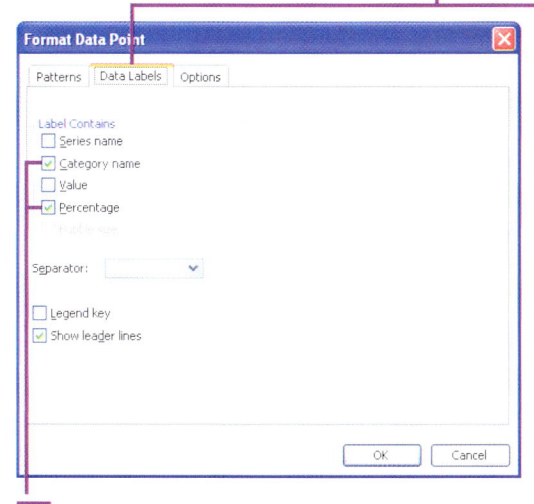

4 In Windows, turn on the check boxes for Category name and Percentage…

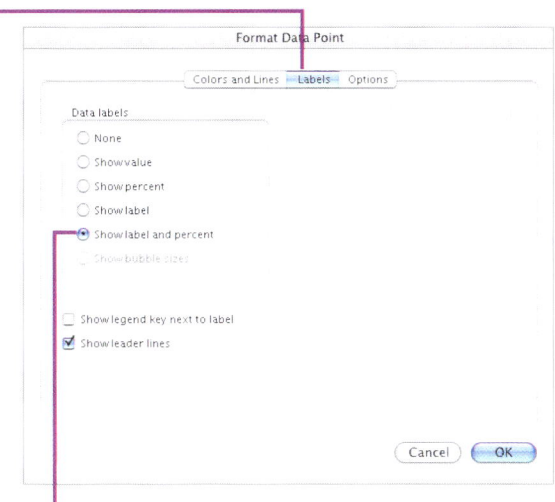

…or in Mac OS, select Show label and percent.

add a chart   **99**

add data labels (cont'd)

5 Click OK.

The name of the category and its percentage appear beside the pie piece.

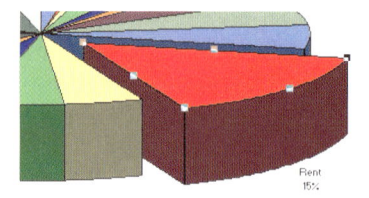

6 Repeat steps 1 through 5 for Utilities and Annual Party.

When you're finished, the pie chart should look like this.

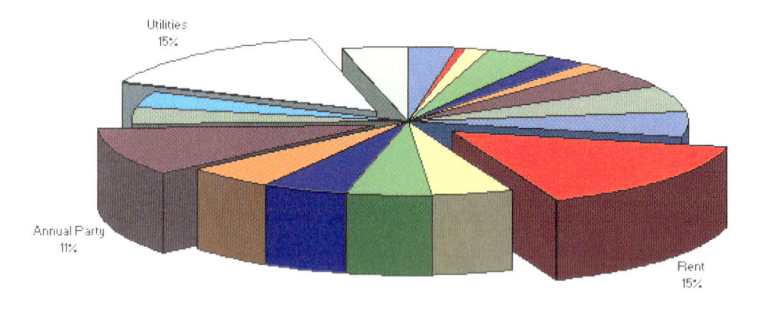

Save your work.

Click the Save button on the Standard toolbar.

100   **add a chart**

extra bits

select a chart type p. 92

- If you point to the Press and Hold to View Sample button and hold the mouse button down, you can view a sample of the chart type you selected with your data plotted.

set chart options pp. 94-95

- The number and type of options that appear in Step 3 of the Chart Wizard vary depending on the type of chart you selected in Step 1.
- The position of a chart's legend will impact the size of the chart. You can see this for yourself by trying different Placement settings for the legend.

add data labels pp. 99-100

- If you wanted data labels to appear for all pieces of the pie, you could set Data Label options in Step 3 of the Chart Wizard, as shown on page 95.

add a chart **101**

8. print your work

In many instances, when you're finished creating and formatting a worksheet or chart, you'll need to print it.

Although you can just use the Print command (or toolbar button) to send a sheet to your printer for hard copy, Excel offers a wide variety of page setup options you can use to customize your printout. For example, you can change page orientation and scaling, set margins, add headers and footers, and specify a print area. All of these settings affect the way your sheet will appear when printed. Fortunately, Excel's Print Preview feature (shown here) enables you to see what your sheets will look like before you print them, so you can fine-tune their appearance without wasting a lot of paper.

This chapter explores many of Excel's page setup options to prepare our worksheets for printing and to print them.

select the sheets

To print a sheet or set print options for it, you must activate it. Because our workbook includes several worksheets which will all have the same settings, we can select them all and set options for all of them at once.

1 Click the sheet tab for the January sheet.

2 Hold down the Control (Windows) or Command (Mac OS) key and click the sheet tabs for the Feburary, March, and Quarter 1 sheets.

All of the sheet tabs you clicked become selected.

104   print your work

open page setup

The Page Setup dialog is a goldmine of options for setting up worksheets and charts for printing. Its options are organized into five categories:

- Page options control page orientation and scaling.

- Margins options control margin measurements and the centering of the sheet on the page.

- Header/Footer options enable you to choose from predefined headers or footers or create your own.

- Sheet options (which appear for worksheets only) enable you to specify what prints and how it prints.

- Chart options (which appear for chart sheets only) enable you to specify how a chart will print.

This chapter explores some of these options. But first, let's open that dialog.

Choose Page Setup from the File menu.

Windows

Mac OS

print your work   105

set page options (Windows)

Page options affect page orientation and scaling, as well as a few other settings. We'll set Page options for Portrait orientation, 100% scaling, and Letter size paper. These options should be set by default, but we'll check them, just in case they aren't.

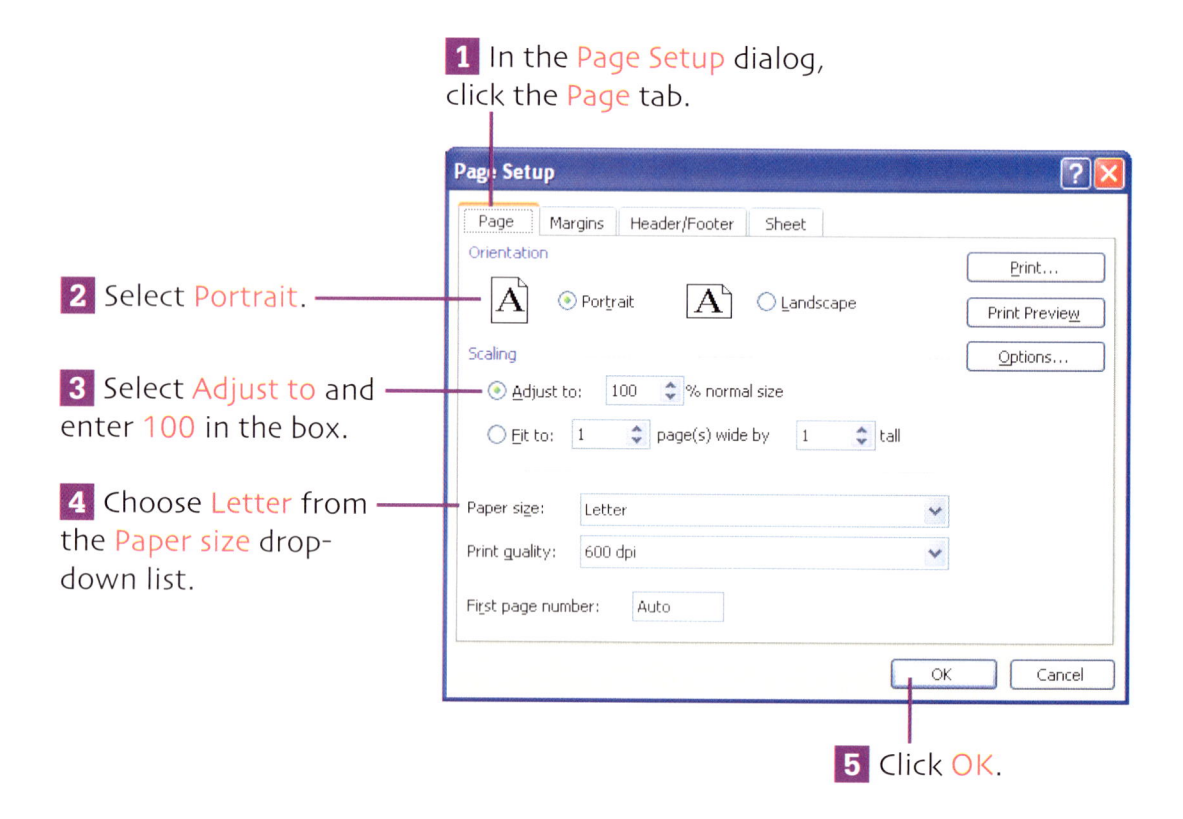

1 In the Page Setup dialog, click the Page tab.

2 Select Portrait.

3 Select Adjust to and enter 100 in the box.

4 Choose Letter from the Paper size drop-down list.

5 Click OK.

106   print your work

set page options (Mac OS)

Page options affect page orientation and scaling, as well as a few other settings. We'll set Page options for Portrait orientation, 100% scaling, and Letter size paper. These options should be set by default, but we'll check them, just in case they aren't.

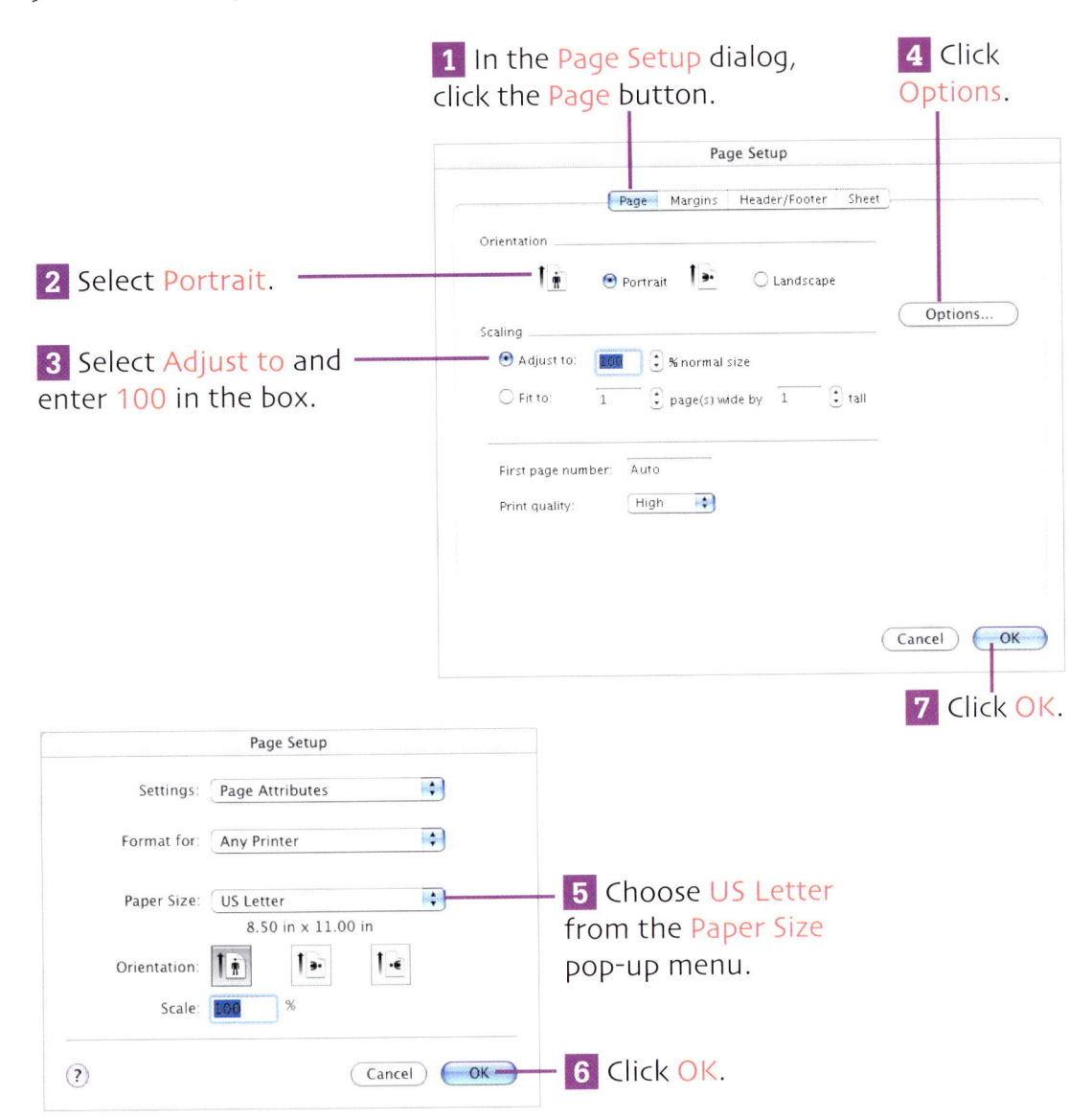

1 In the Page Setup dialog, click the Page button.

2 Select Portrait.

3 Select Adjust to and enter 100 in the box.

4 Click Options.

7 Click OK.

5 Choose US Letter from the Paper Size pop-up menu.

6 Click OK.

print your work   **107**

adjust margins

A margin is the amount of space between the printable area on a page and the edge of the paper. In Excel, Margins options enable you to control the space between the edge of the paper and the sheet contents, as well as the header or footer. Margins settings also enable you to center a sheet horizontally or vertically on a page.

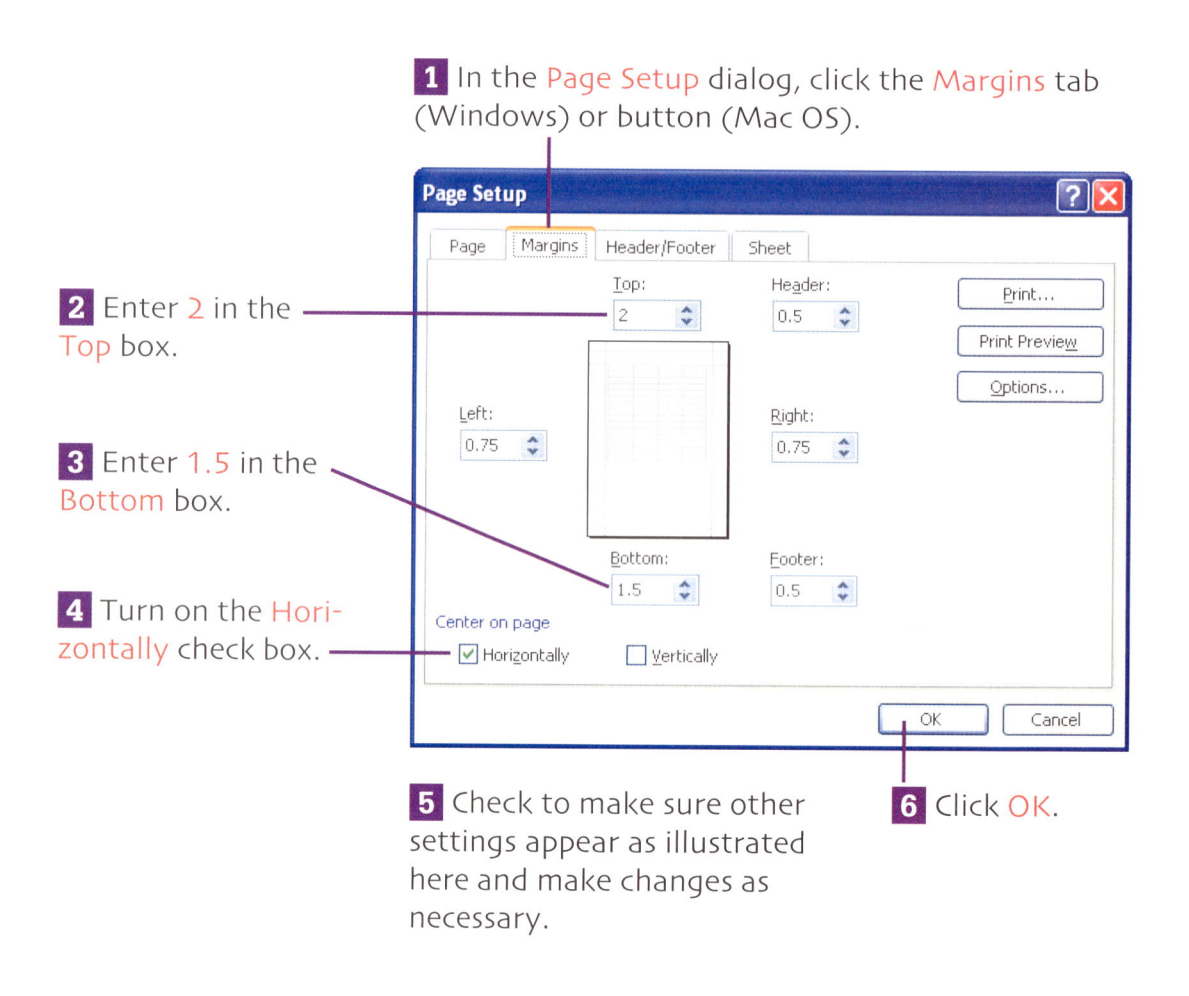

1 In the Page Setup dialog, click the Margins tab (Windows) or button (Mac OS).

2 Enter 2 in the Top box.

3 Enter 1.5 in the Bottom box.

4 Turn on the Horizontally check box.

5 Check to make sure other settings appear as illustrated here and make changes as necessary.

6 Click OK.

add a standard footer

A footer is text that appears at the bottom of every page. In Excel, you add a footer with the Header/Footer options of the Page Setup dialog, which gives you a choice of predefined or custom headers and footers. For our example, we'll add a standard, predefined footer.

1 In the Page Setup dialog, click the Header/Footer tab (Windows) or button (Mac OS).

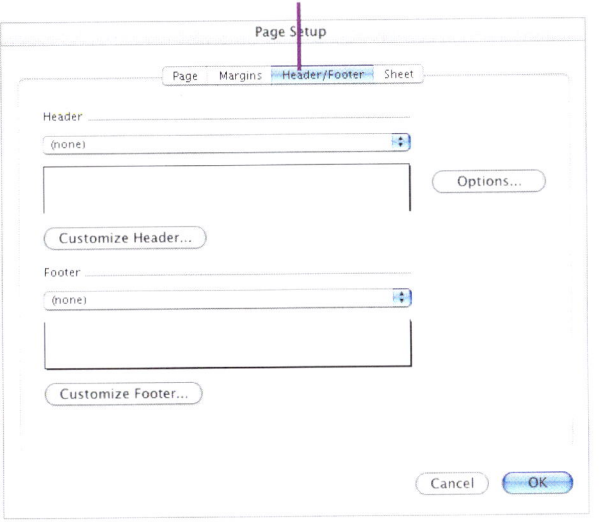

2 Choose the fifth option on the drop-down list (Windows) or pop-up menu (Mac OS) under Footer. It should display your company name followed by the word Confidential, the current date, and Page 1.

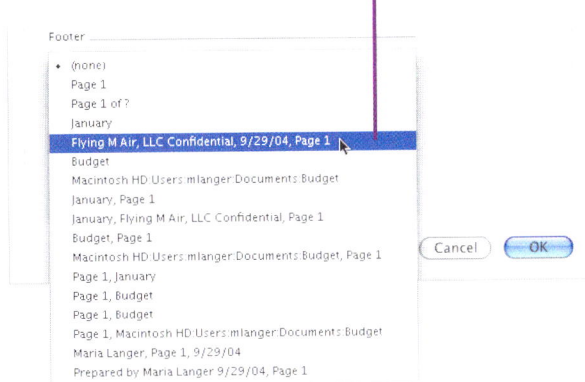

The footer appears in the Footer preview area.

print your work 109

add a custom header

A header is text that appears at the top of every page. In Excel, you add a header with the Header/Footer options of the Page Setup dialog, which gives you a choice of predefined or custom headers and footers. For our example, we'll add a custom header.

1 In the Page Setup dialog, click the Header/Footer tab (Windows) or button (Mac OS).

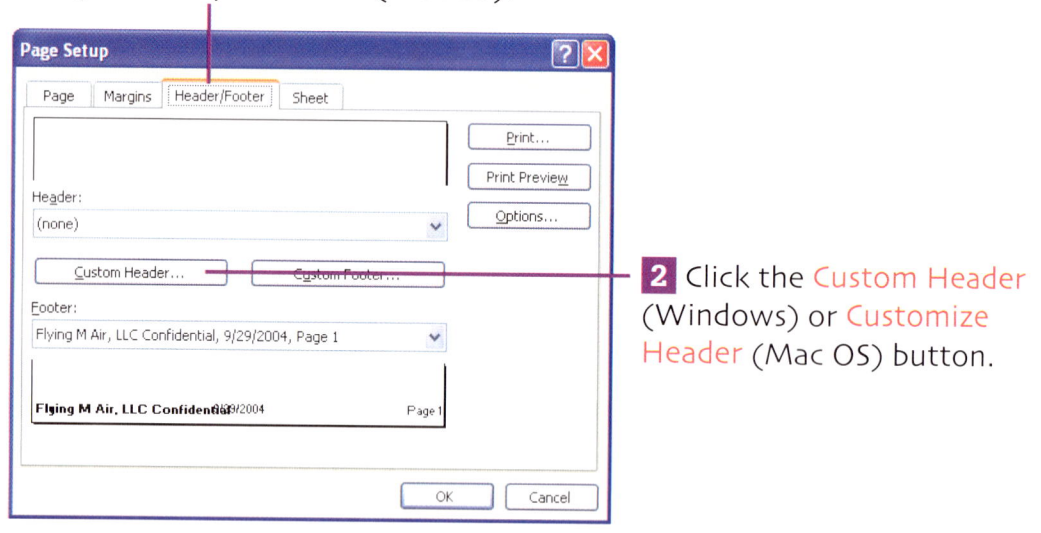

2 Click the Custom Header (Windows) or Customize Header (Mac OS) button.

The Header dialog appears.

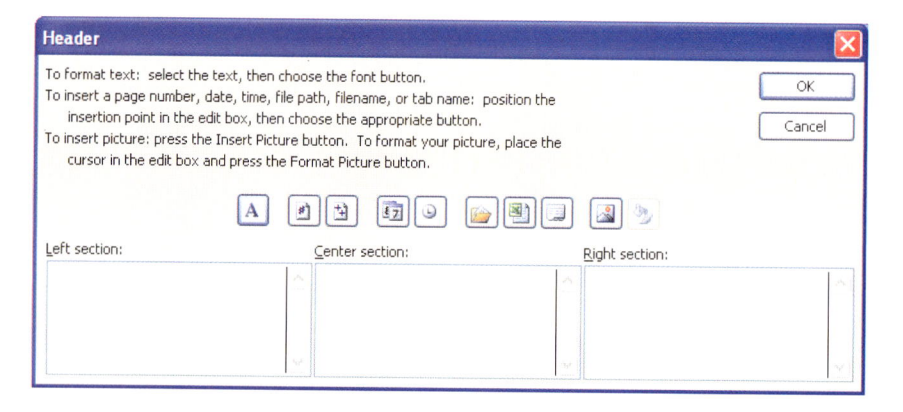

110 print your work

3 In the Left section box, type File Name: and press Enter (Windows) or Return (Mac OS).

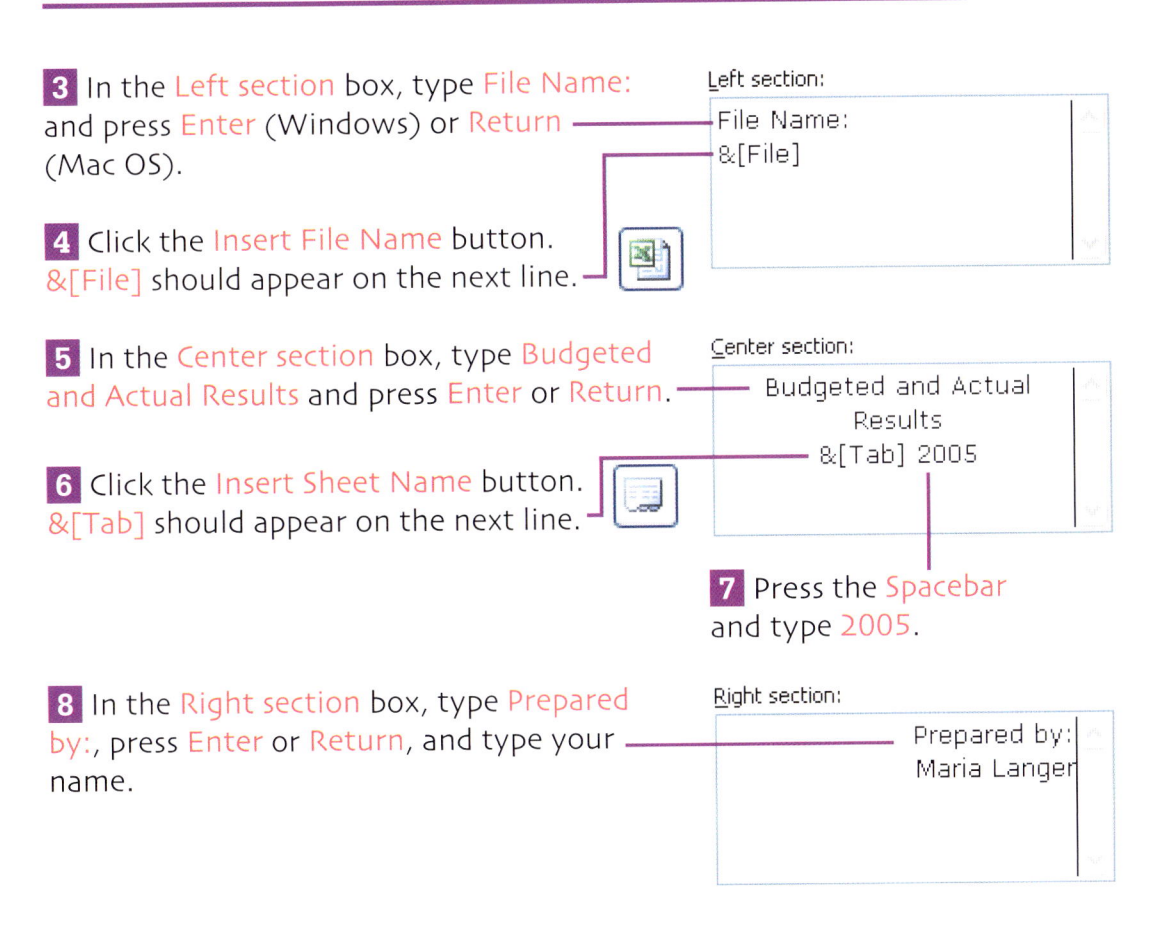

Left section:
File Name:
&[File]

4 Click the Insert File Name button. &[File] should appear on the next line.

5 In the Center section box, type Budgeted and Actual Results and press Enter or Return.

Center section:
Budgeted and Actual Results
&[Tab] 2005

6 Click the Insert Sheet Name button. &[Tab] should appear on the next line.

7 Press the Spacebar and type 2005.

8 In the Right section box, type Prepared by:, press Enter or Return, and type your name.

Right section:
Prepared by:
Maria Langer

At this point, the Header dialog should look like this.

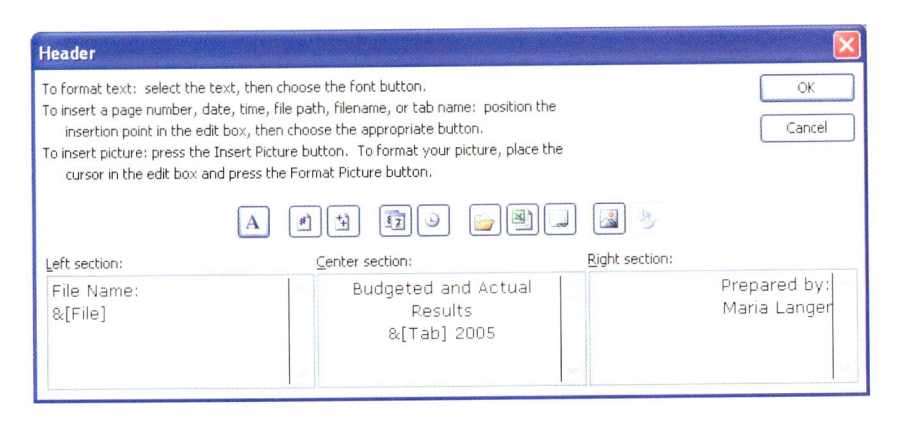

Header

To format text: select the text, then choose the font button.
To insert a page number, date, time, file path, filename, or tab name: position the insertion point in the edit box, then choose the appropriate button.
To insert picture: press the Insert Picture button. To format your picture, place the cursor in the edit box and press the Format Picture button.

Left section:
File Name:
&[File]

Center section:
Budgeted and Actual Results
&[Tab] 2005

Right section:
Prepared by:
Maria Langer

print your work   **111**

add custom header (cont'd)

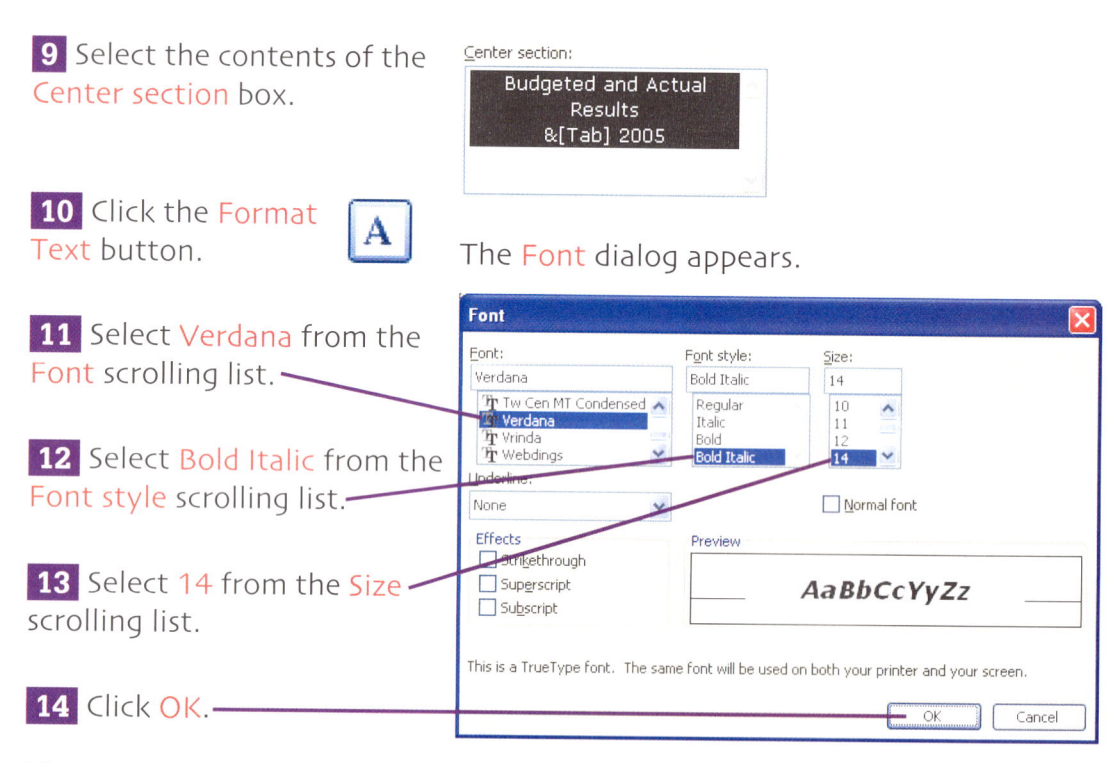

9 Select the contents of the Center section box.

10 Click the Format Text button.

The Font dialog appears.

11 Select Verdana from the Font scrolling list.

12 Select Bold Italic from the Font style scrolling list.

13 Select 14 from the Size scrolling list.

14 Click OK.

The Center section text is formatted to your specifications.

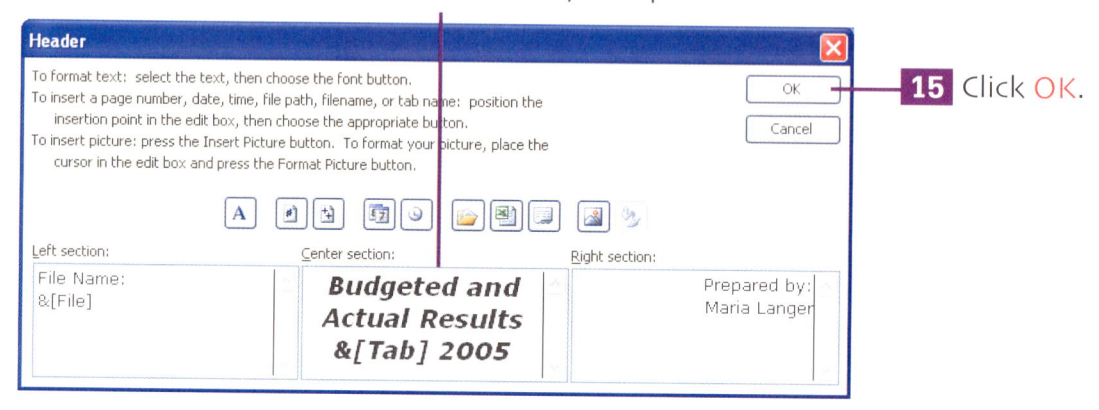

15 Click OK.

Your custom header appears in the Header preview area.

112 **print your work**

save settings

We've made a bunch of changes in the Page Setup dialog. It's time to save them.

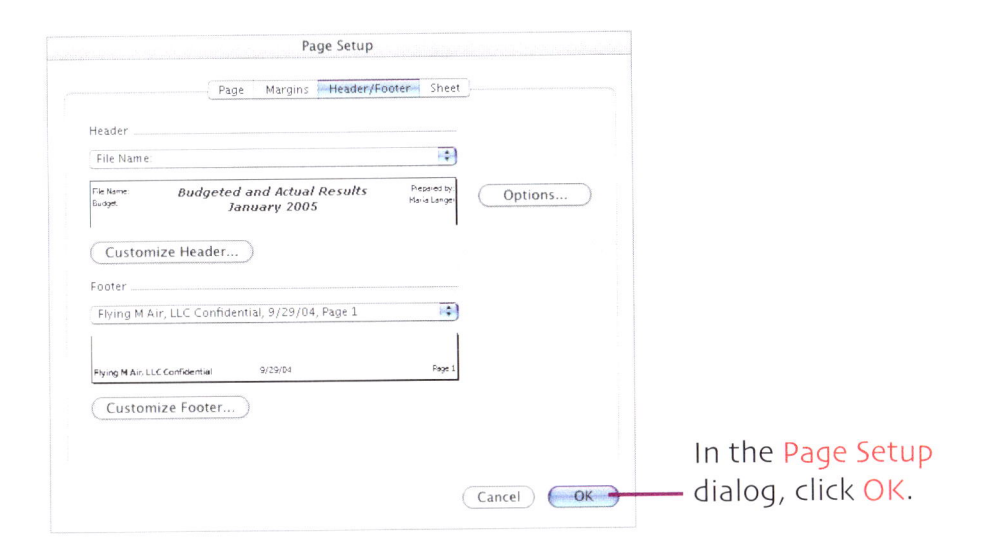

In the Page Setup dialog, click OK.

Save your work.

Click the Save button on the Standard toolbar.

print your work 113

preview the sheets (Win)

Excel's Print Preview feature saves time and paper by enabling you to see what a document will look like on paper without actually printing it. If it looks good, you can click a Print button to send it to your printer. If it doesn't look good, you can click a Setup button to go back to the Page Setup dialog and fix it.

Click the Print Preview button on the Standard toolbar.

A Print Preview window opens.

Click Print to open the Print dialog.

Click Setup to open the Page Setup dialog.

Click Close to close the window.

Click Next or Previous to scroll through pages.

Number of pages in printout.

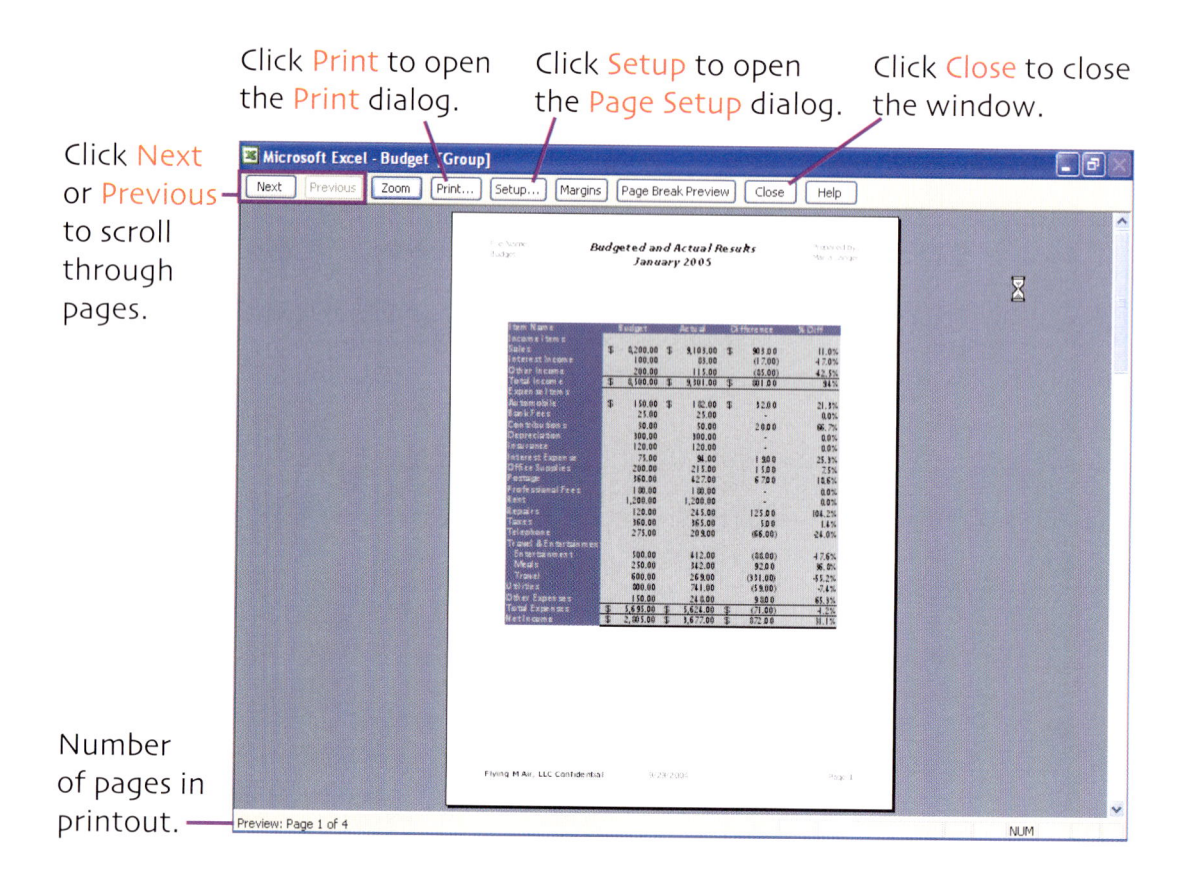

114

print your work

preview the sheets (Mac)

Excel's Print Preview feature saves time and paper by enabling you to see what a document will look like on paper without actually printing it. If it looks good, you can click a Print button to send it to your printer. If it doesn't look good, you can click a Setup button to go back to the Page Setup dialog and fix it.

Click the Print Preview button on the Standard toolbar.

A Print Preview window opens.

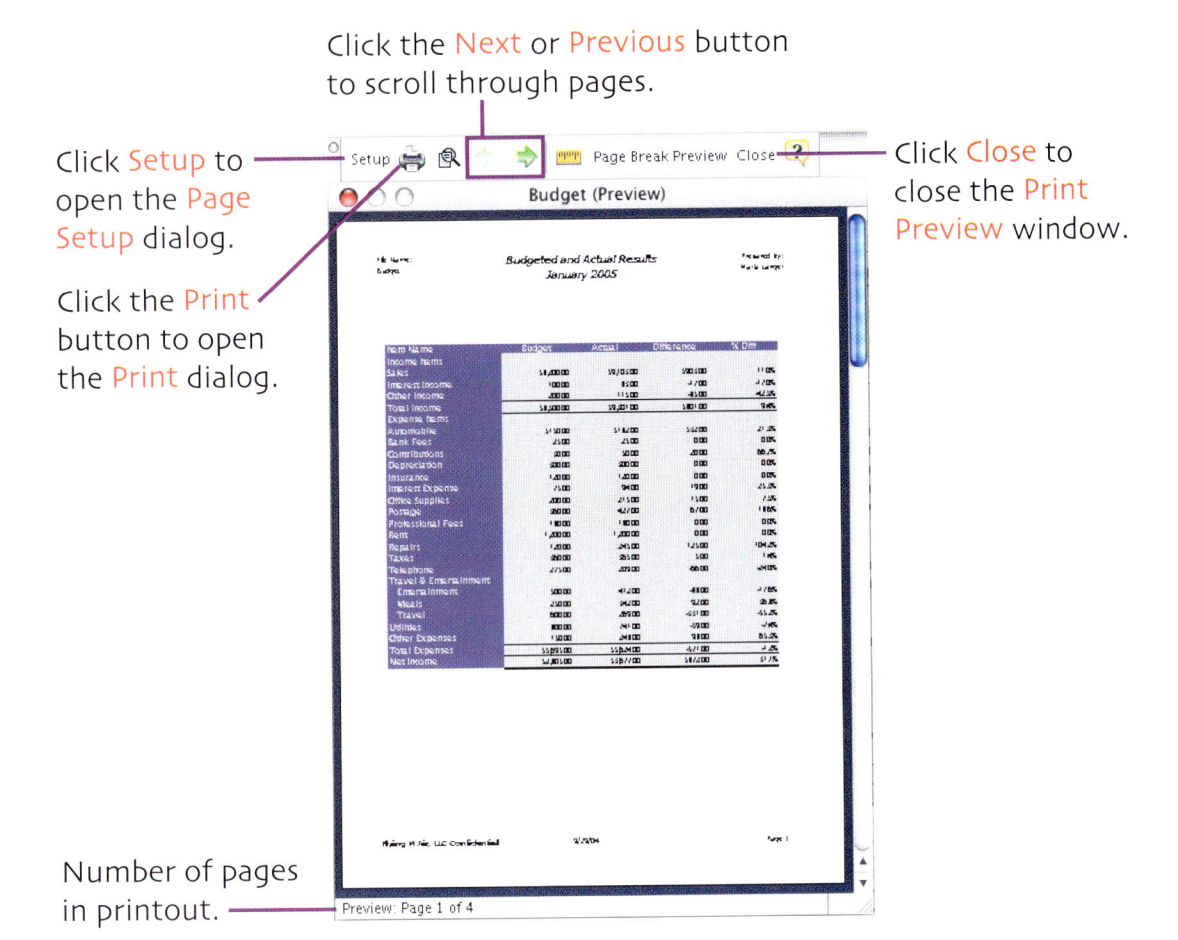

Click the Next or Previous button to scroll through pages.

Click Setup to open the Page Setup dialog.

Click the Print button to open the Print dialog.

Click Close to close the Print Preview window.

Number of pages in printout.

print your work 115

print your work (Windows)

Once you're satisfied that the worksheets will look good on paper, you can print them.

1 Choose Print from the File menu.

The Print dialog appears.

2 Choose a printer from the Name drop-down list.

3 Select All in the Print range area.

4 Select Active sheet(s) in the Print what area.

5 Enter 1 in the Number of copies box.

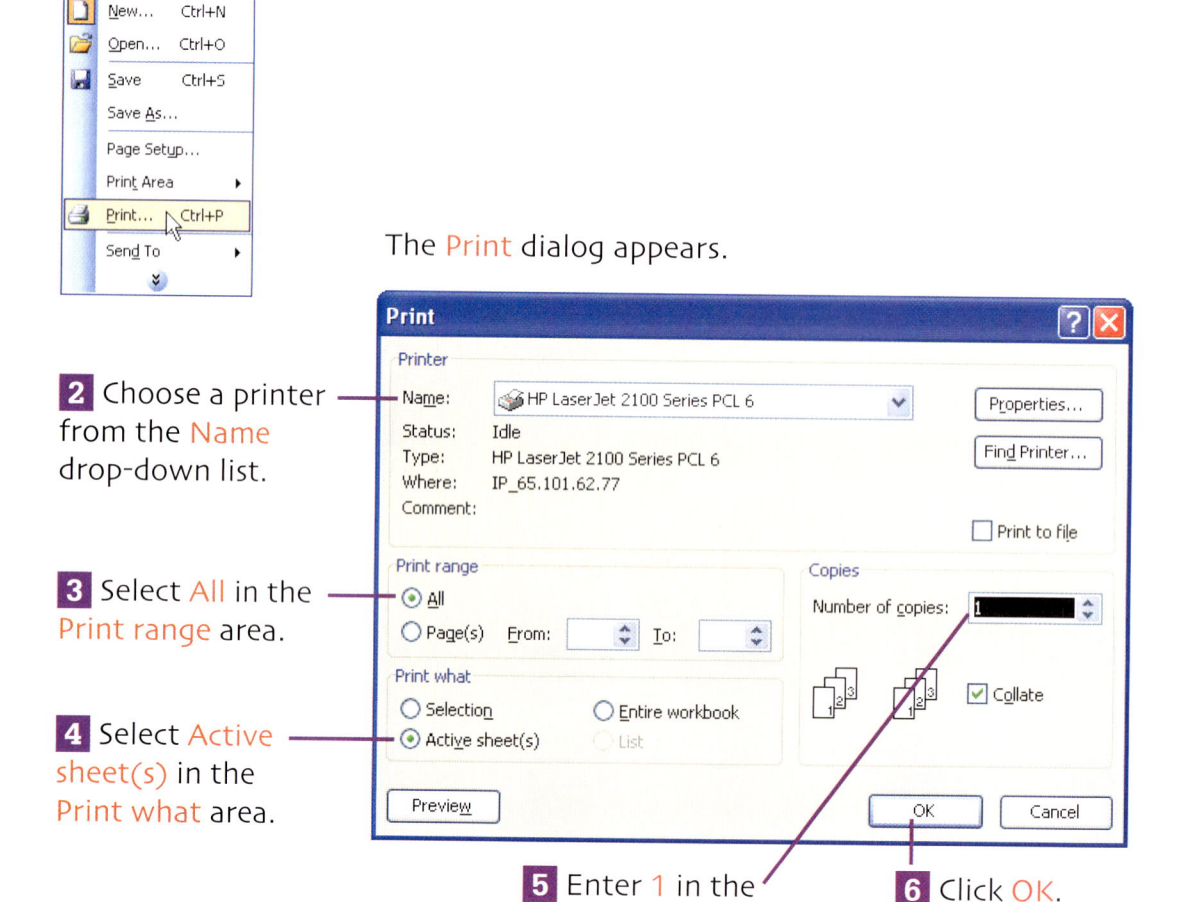

6 Click OK.

The worksheets are sent to the printer where they print.

116

print your work

print your work (Mac OS)

Once you're satisfied that the worksheets will look good on paper, you can print them.

1 Choose **Print** from the **File** menu.

The **Print** dialog appears.

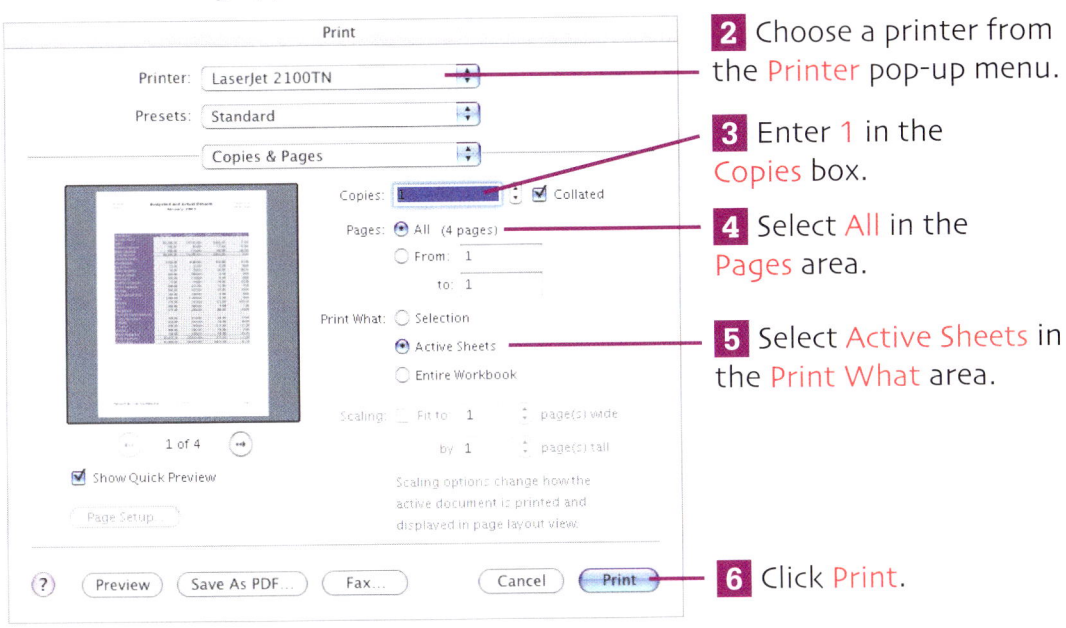

2 Choose a printer from the **Printer** pop-up menu.

3 Enter **1** in the **Copies** box.

4 Select **All** in the **Pages** area.

5 Select **Active Sheets** in the **Print What** area.

6 Click **Print**.

The worksheets are sent to the printer where they print.

print your work   **117**

extra bits

set page options pp. 106–107

- If you discover, when previewing your worksheet, that it doesn't quite fit on a single page, you can force it to fit on that page. Select Fit to in the Page options of the Page Setup dialog and make sure 1 is entered in both boxes beside it.

add a standard footer p. 109

- Excel gets your company name from information you entered when you installed it.

add a custom header pp. 110–112

- Excel left-aligns the Left section text, centers the Center section text, and right-aligns the Right section text.
- It isn't necessary to enter text in all three sections of a custom header or footer. Just use the sections you need.

save settings p. 113

- Page Setup options are automatically saved with a workbook file when you save the workbook. So once you've set options for a file, you don't have to reset them unless you want to change them.

print your work pp. 116–117

- Clicking the Print button on the Standard toolbar sends the selected sheets to the printer without displaying the Print dialog.
- In Windows, clicking the Properties button in the Print dialog displays additional options that are specific to your printer. Consult the manual that came with your printer for additional information about these options.

index

= (equals sign), formulas, 45
10 point Arial font, 70
10 point Verdana font, 70

A

activating cells, 27, 44
active cell
    Mac interface, 6
    Windows interface, 5
active sheets, 24
addressing worksheets, 25
Align Center button, 78
Align Right button, 87
alignment
    column headings, 87
    formatting, 78
Alignment and Spacing area, Formatting Palette
    Align Center button, 78
    Indent box, 79
All Programs command (Start menu), 4
All reference box, Consolidate dialog, 62–64
Append file extension check box, 21
Apple menu commands, System Preferences, 14
Apple Pro Mouse, 3
arrow keys, activating cells, 27
arrow pointing down, 3
author Web site, xiv
Auto Fill Options button, 40, 46
AutoComplete feature, 44
AutoFit feature, 76
automatic error-checking feature, 57
automatic rewriting formulas, 57
AutoSum button, 35

B

Bold button, 70
borders, formatting, 80–81
Borders and Shading area, Formatting Palette
    Color button, 82
    Type button, 80–81
Borders button, 80–81
budget worksheets, 23
    activating cells, 27, 44
    budget, 23
    calculations
        differences, 33
        net income, 37
        percent differences, 34
        sums, 35–36
column
    headings, 29
    widths, 30, 44
copying, 39
    fill handles, 40–42
    formulas, 38
entering information, 26
naming sheet, 24, 44
pasting, 39
references, 25
row headings, 28
    AutoComplete feature, 44
values
    changing, 43
    deleting, 47
    entering, 31–32, 44–45
buttons
    dialogs, 11
    mouse, 3

C

calculations
    consolidation feature, 66–67
    differences, 33
    net income, 37
    percent differences, 34
    sums, 35–36
case-sensitivity, 45

119

index

Category list, Format Cells dialog, 72
Category Name check box, 99
cells, 23
    activating, 27, 44
    formatting
        alignment, 78
        borders, 80–81
        column width, 76–77
        font, 70–71, 86
        shading, 82–83
        text, 79, 84
        underlines, 87
    gridlines, 87
    pointer
        Mac interface, 6
        Windows interface, 5
    values
        changing, 43
        clearing, 51–52
        deleting, 47
        entering, 31–32, 44–45
        formatting, 72–73, 86
Cells command (Format menu), 72, 86
Center button, 78
Chart options, Page Setup dialog, 105
Chart subtype area, 92
Chart title box, 94
Chart type list, 92
Chart Wizard, 89. See also charts
    chart type selection, 92
    checking source data, 93
    location setting, 96
    option setting, 94–95
    starting, 91

Chart Wizard button, 91
Chart Wizard dialog, 91
charts. See also Chart Wizard
    checking source data, 93
    data labels, 99–101
    hiding rows, 90
    location setting, 96
    option setting, 94–95, 101
    pie exploding, 97–98
    sheet, 15, 89
    starting Chart Wizard, 91
    type selection, 92, 101
check boxes
    dialogs, 11
    selecting, 14
Clear command (Edit menu), 51
Clear submenu, 51
clicks, 3
    activating cells, 27
Color button, 82
color formatting
    shading, 82–83
    text, 84
Column command (Format menu), 77
Column Width dialog, 77
columns, 23
    heading, 29
        alignment, 87
        Mac interface, 6
        Windows interface, 5
    widths, 30, 44
        formatting, 76–77
Columns command (Insert menu), 57
comma formatting, 86

Comma Style button, 72, 86
Command-S shortcut key (Save command), 14
commands
    Apple menu, System Preferences, 14
    Data menu, Consolidate, 61
    Edit menu
        Clear, 51
        Copy, 39
        Delete, 54, 57
        Paste, 39
    Excel menu
        Preferences, 18, 21
        Quit Excel, 12
    File menu
        Exit, 12
        Page Setup, 105
        Print, 116–117
        Save, 19–20
        Save As, 21
    Format menu
        Cells, 72, 86
        Column, 77
        Row, 90
    Insert menu
        Columns, 57
        Rows, 53, 57
    menus, 9
    Start menu, All Programs, 4
    Tools menu, Options, 17
    View menu
        Formula Bar, 14
        Toolbars, 10
Consolidate command (Data menu), 61
Consolidate dialog, 61–64
consolidation feature, 59, 61–64, 67

percent difference
  calculation, 66–67
 sheet preparation, 60
 verifying, 65
contextual menus, 9
Control key (Mac), contextual menus, 9
Copy command (Edit menu), 39
copying, 39
 duplicating worksheets, 50
 fill handles, 40–42
 formulas, 38
creating workbook files, 16
 Mac view preferences, 21
cross pointers, 3
Ctrl-S shortcut key (Save command), 14
Currency button, 73
currency formatting, 86
Custom Header button, 110
Customize Header button, 110
customizing, Mac scroll bars, 14

D

data, charts, 93
 labels, 99–101
Data Labels tab, 95
Data menu commands, Consolidate, 61
Data range box, 93
Decrease Decimal button, 75
Delete command (Edit menu), 54, 57

deleting
 rows, 54
 values, 47
dialogs, 11
 Chart Wizard, 91
 Column Width, 77
 Consolidate, 61–64
 Font, 112
 Format Cells, 72, 86
 Format Data Point, 99
 Format Data Series, 99
 Header, 110–112
 Options (Windows), 17
 Page Setup
  adjusting margins, 108
  custom headers, 110–112, 118
  opening, 105
  saving, 113
  setting page options, 106–107, 118
  standard footers, 109, 118
 Preferences (Mac), 18
 Print dialog, 116–117
 Save As, 19–20, 21
document icons, 2
Documents folder (Mac), saving workbook file, 20
double-clicks, 3
down scroll arrows, 8
dragging, 3
drop-down lists (Windows), dialogs, 11
duplicating worksheets, 49
 clearing values, 51–52
 copying sheet, 50

deleting rows, 54
entering new values, 56
inserting rows, 53

E

Edit menu commands
 Clear, 51
 Copy, 39
 Delete, 54, 57
 Paste, 39
embedded charts, 89
entry selection areas, 31
equals sign (=), formulas, 45
errors, formulas, 45–46
Excel menu commands
 Preferences, 18, 21
 Quit Excel, 12
Excel program icons, 2
Exit command (File menu), 12
exiting Excel, 12

F

Fehily, Chris, Windows XP: Visual QuickStart Guide, 2
File menu commands
 Exit, 12
 Page Setup, 105
 Print, 116–117
 Save, 19–20
 Save As, 21
File name box, Save As dialog, 19
Fill button, 82
fill handles, copying contents, 40–42

index **121**

index

Finder, 2
Fit to Page option, Page Setup dialog, 118
Font area, Formatting Palette, Color button, 84
Font Color button, 84
Font dialog, 112
Font drop-down list, 71
Font Scrolling list, Font dialog, 112
Font Size drop-down list, 70
Font Style Scrolling list, Font dialog, 112
fonts, formatting, 70–71, 86
footers, 109, 118
Format Cells dialog, 72, 86
Format Data Point dialog, 99
Format Data Series dialog, 99
Format menu commands
　Cells, 72, 86
　Column, 77
　Row, 90
Format pop-up menu, 20
Format Text button, 112
formatting, 69
　alignment, 78
　borders, 80–81
　column width, 76–77
　comma, 86
　currency, 86
　font, 70–71, 86
　multiple sheets, 85
　percentages, 74–75
　shading, 82–83
　text
　　color, 84

indent, 79
underlines, 87
values, 72–73, 86
Formatting Palette, 10
　Alignment and Spacing area
　　Align Center button, 78
　　Indent box, 79
　　Bold button, 70
　Borders and Shading area
　　Color button, 82
　　Type button, 80–81
　Decrease Decimal button, 75
　Font area, Color button, 84
　Font drop-down list, 71
　Font Size drop-down list, 70
　Format drop-down list, 73
　Formatting drop-down list
　　Currency, 73
　　Percentage, 74
　Mac interface, 6
Formatting toolbar, 10
　Bold button, 70
　Borders button, 80–81
　Center button, 78
　Comma Style button, 72, 86
　Currency button, 73
　Fill button, 82
　Font Color button, 84
　Font drop-down list, 71
　Font Size drop-down list, 70
　Increase Decimal button, 75
　Increase Indent button, 79
　Percent Style button, 74
　Windows interface, 5

Formula Bar command (View menu), 14
formulas
　automatic rewrite, 57
　bar, 65
　　Mac interface, 6
　　Mac workbook file view preferences, 21
　　Windows interface, 5
　copying, 38–39
　equals sign (=), 45
　pasting, 39
　sum calculations, 36
　worksheet information, 26
function tooltip, calculating sums, 35–36

G

gridlines, cells, 87

H

hard disk icon, 4
Header dialog, 110–112
Header preview area, 112
Header/Footer options, Page Setup dialog, 105
Header/Footer tab, 109–110
headers, 110–112, 118
headings
　columns, 29
　　alignment, 87
　rows, 28
　　AutoComplete feature, 44

Mac interface, 6
Windows interface, 5
Hide command (Format menu), 90
hiding rows, 90
Home folder (Mac), saving workbook file, 20

I

icons, 2
income calculations, 37
Increase Decimal button, 75
Increase Indent button, 79
Indent box, 79
indent text, formatting, 79
information, entering in worksheets, 26
Insert File Name button, 111
Insert menu commands
　Columns, 57
　Rows, 53, 57
Insert Sheet Name button, 111
inserting rows, 53
interface elements, 5–6

L

Label Contains area check boxes, 95
labels
　chart data, 99–100
　worksheet information, 26
Legend tab, 94
Lucinda Sans font, 71

M

Mac
　10 point Verdana font, 70
　changing views, 14
　column widths, 86
　creating blank workbook file, 16
　　setting view preferences, 21
　dialogs, 11
　Finder, 2
　formatting borders, 80–81
　formatting text color, 84
　interface elements, 5
　mouse buttons, 3, 13
　naming sheets, 24
　opening program, 4
　percentage formatting, 74–75
　previewing sheets, 115
　printing, 117
　quitting Excel, 12
　saving workbook files, 20
　　sharing with Windows user, 21
　scroll bars, 8
　　customizing, 14
　setting page options, 107
　views, 7
Mac OS X Panther: Visual QuickStart Guide, 2
margins, 108
Margins option, Page Setup dialog, 105
Margins tab, 108
menus, 9

bar
　Mac interface, 6
　Windows interface, 5
Microsoft Excel X for Macintosh: Visual QuickStart Guide, xv
Microsoft Office command (Start menu), 4
Microsoft Office Excel 2003 command (Start menu), 4
Microsoft Office Excel 2003 for Windows: Visual QuickStart Guide, xv
mouse, 3, 13
My Documents button, 19
My Documents folder (Windows), 19

N

naming worksheets, 24, 44
net income calculations, 37
New button, creating workbook file, 16
Normal view, 7
Normal View button (Mac), 16
Normal View icon (Mac), 14
Number button, 72

O

opening program, 4, 13
option buttons (Windows), dialogs, 11
Options command (Tools menu), 17
Options dialog (Windows), 17
outline symbol, 65

index

P

Page Break Preview view, 7
Page button, 106
Page Layout view
    changing to Normal view, 14
    Mac, 7
Page options, Page Setup dialog, 105
Page Setup command (File menu), 105
Page Setup dialog
    adjusting margins, 108
    custom headers, 110–112, 118
    opening, 105
    saving, 113
    setting page options, 106–107, 118
    standard footers, 109, 118
Page tab, 106
Paper Size pop-up menu, 107
Paste command (Edit menu), 39
Paste Options button, 39
pasting, 39
Percent Style button, 74
Percentage check box, 99
percentages
    differences, 34
        consolidation feature, 66–67
    formatting, 74–75
pie charts, 97–98
pointers
    activating cells, 27
    mouse, 3

points, font, 86
pop-up menus (Mac), dialogs, 11
Preferences command (Excel menu), 18, 21
Preferences dialog (Mac), 18
Press and Hold to View Sample button, 101
previewing sheets
    Mac, 115
    Windows, 114
Print command (File menu), 116–117
Print dialog, 116–117
Print Preview button, 103, 114–115
Print Preview window, 114
Print range area, 116
Print What area, 117
printing
    Mac, 117
    Page Setup
        adjusting margins, 108
        custom headers, 110–112, 118
        opening, 105
        saving, 113
        setting page options, 106–107, 118
        standard footers, 109, 118
    previewing sheets
        Mac, 115
        Windows, 114
    Print Preview, 103
    sheet selection, 104
    Windows, 116
program icons, 2

Project Gallery, 4
Properties button, Print dialog, 118
push buttons, dialogs, 11

Q

Quit Excel command (Excel menu), 12
quitting Excel, 12

R

radio buttons (Mac)
    dialogs, 11
    selecting, 14
Reference box, Consolidate dialog, 62–64
references, worksheets, 25
right arrow keys, activating cells, 27
right-clicks (Windows), 3
    contextual menus, 9
rollers, mouse, 13
Row command (Format menu), 90
rows, 23
    deleting, 54
    heading, 28
        AutoComplete feature, 44
        Mac interface, 6
        Windows interface, 5
    hiding, 90
    inserting, 53
Rows command (Insert menu), 53, 57

S

Save As command (File menu), 21
Save As dialog, 19–20, 21
Save as type drop-down list, 19
Save button, Standard toolbar, 21
Save command (File menu), 19–20
   shortcut keys, 14
saving, Page Setup dialog, 113
saving workbook files, 19–20
scroll bars
   customizing Mac, 14
   Mac interface, 6
   windows, 8
   Windows interface, 5
scroll box, 8
scrolling lists, dialogs, 11
Select All button, 71
shading, formatting, 82–83
Sheet options, Page Setup dialog, 105
sheets, 15
   activating cells, 27, 44
   budget, 23
   calculations
      differences, 33
      net income, 37
      percent differences, 34
      sums, 35–36
   column
      headings, 29
      widths, 30, 44
   consolidation feature, 59, 61–64, 67
      percent difference calculation, 66–67
      sheet preparation, 60
      verifying, 65
   copying, 39
      fill handles, 40–42
      formulas, 38
   duplicating, 49
      clearing values, 51–52
      copying sheet, 50
      deleting rows, 54
      entering new values, 56
      inserting rows, 53
   entering information, 26
   formatting. See formatting
   naming sheet, 24, 44
   pasting, 39
   previewing
      Mac, 115
      Windows, 114
   printing, 104
   references, 25
   row headings, 28
      AutoComplete feature, 44
   tabs, 24
      changing sheet position, 57
      Mac interface, 6
      Windows interface, 5
   values
      changing, 43
      deleting, 47
      entering, 31–32, 44–45
   window
      Mac interface, 6
      Windows interface, 5
   workbook files, 15
shortcut keys, menu commands, 14
shortcut menus, 14
Show label and percent check box, 99
Show legend check box, 94
Sidebar, saving workbook file, 20
spreadsheets, 15
   activating cells, 27, 44
   budget, 23
   calculations
      differences, 33
      net income, 37
      percent differences, 34
      sums, 35–36
   column
      headings, 29
      widths, 30, 44
   consolidation feature, 59, 61–64, 67
      percent difference calculation, 66–67
      sheet preparation, 60
      verifying, 65
   copying, 39
      fill handles, 40–42
      formulas, 38
   duplicating, 49
      clearing values, 51–52
      copying sheet, 50
      deleting rows, 54
      entering new values, 56
      inserting rows, 53
   entering information, 26
   formatting. See formatting
   naming sheet, 24, 44
   pasting, 39

index

spreadsheets (continued)
  references, 25
  row headings, 28
    AutoComplete feature, 44
  values
    changing, 43
    deleting, 47
    entering, 31–32, 44–45
  window
    Mac interface, 6
    Windows interface, 5
Standard toolbar, 10
  AutoSum button, 35
  Chart Wizard button, 91
  Mac interface, 6
  New button, 16
  Print Preview button, 114–115
  Save button, 21
  Windows interface, 5
Start menu commands, All Programs, 4
starting Excel, 4, 13
status bar
  Mac interface, 6
  Windows interface, 5
submenus, 9
sum calculations, 35–36
SUM function, 35, 45
System Preferences command (Apple menu), 14

T

tabs
  dialogs, 11
  sheets, 24

Task Pane, Windows interface, 5
terms, 2
text
  boxes, dialogs, 11
  formatting
    color, 84
    headers, 112
    indent, 79
title bar
  Mac interface, 6
  Windows interface, 5
toolbars, 10
  displaying on separate lines, 14
Toolbars command (View menu), 10
Tools menu commands, Options, 17
Top and Bottom Border button, 80–81
Type button, 80–81
typeface, 86

U

underlines, 87
up arrow keys, activating cells, 27
up scroll arrows, 8

V

values
  changing, 43
  clearing, 51–52
  deleting, 47

entering
  duplicated worksheet, 56
  in worksheets, 31–32, 44–45
  formatting, 72–73, 86
  worksheet information, 26
View buttons (Mac), changing view, 7
View menu
  changing view, 7
  commands
    Formula Bar, 14
    Toolbars, 10
View tab, Options dialog (Windows), 17
views
  changing, 7
  icons (Mac interface), 6
  Mac view preferences, 18
  Windows view options, 17

W

Web sites, author, xiv
Width command (Format menu), 77
widths, columns, 30, 44
  formatting, 76–77
Windows
  10 point Arial font, 70
  column widths, 86
  creating blank workbook file, 16
  dialogs, 11
  exiting Excel, 12
  formatting borders, 80–81
  formatting text color, 84
  interface elements, 5

mouse buttons, 3, 13
naming sheets, 24
percentage formatting, 74–75
previewing sheets, 114
printing, 116
saving workbook files, 19
scroll bars, 8
setting page options, 106
starting program, 4
views, 7
Windows Explorer, 2
windows scroll bars, 8
Windows XP: Visual QuickStart Guide, 2
workbook files, 15
    creating, 16
    Mac view preferences, 18
    saving, 19–20
    Window view options, 17

worksheets, 15
    activating cells, 27, 44
    budget, 23
    calculations
        differences, 33
        net income, 37
        percent differences, 34
        sums, 35–36
    column
        headings, 29
        widths, 30, 44
    consolidation feature, 59, 61–64, 67
        percent difference calculation, 66–67
        sheet preparation, 60
        verifying, 65
    copying, 39
        fill handles, 40–42
        formulas, 38
    duplicating, 49
        clearing values, 51–52

    copying sheet, 50
    deleting rows, 54
    entering new values, 56
    inserting rows, 53
    entering information, 26
    formatting. See formatting
    naming sheet, 24, 44
    pasting, 39
    references, 25
    row headings, 28
        AutoComplete feature, 44
    tabs, changing sheet position, 57
    values
        changing, 43
        deleting, 47
        entering, 31–32, 44–45
    window
        Mac interface, 6
        Windows interface, 5

Ready to Learn More?

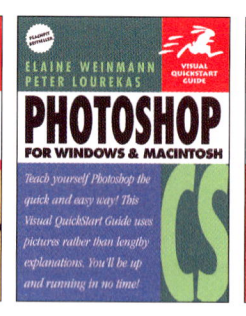

If you enjoyed this project and are ready to learn more, pick up a *Visual QuickStart Guide*, the best-selling, most affordable, most trusted, quick-reference series for computing.

With more than 5.5 million copies in print, *Visual QuickStart Guides* are the industry's best-selling series of affordable, quick-reference guides. This series from Peachpit Press includes more than 200 titles covering the leading applications for digital photography and illustration, digital video and sound editing, Web design and development, business productivity, graphic design, operating systems, and more. Best of all, these books respect your time and intelligence. With tons of well-chosen illustrations and practical, labor-saving tips, they'll have you up to speed on new software fast.

> "When you need to quickly learn to use a new application or new version of an application, you can't do better than the **Visual QuickStart Guides** from Peachpit Press."
> Jay Nelson
> *Design Tools Monthly*

www.peachpit.com